Endorsements

The reasons why Leora wrote and saved what she did, capturing her life and the lives of so many in her bigger circle of family, friends and experiences, may never be fully known. What we do know is that her granddaughter, Joy Neal Kidney, has embraced the role of caretaker and scribe of these records. Kidney continues to transform these archives into a series of vibrant journeys, one book at a time, beckoning others to join her in these reflective adventures.

Leora's Early Years: Guthrie County Roots is the third in this irresistible series. In the wake of Leora's bountiful passage of memorabilia, Joy's meticulous research and gifted writing bring universal understandings alive through the magic of memoir, reminiscence and an intimate examination of everyday folks surviving in bygone times. Relevance for today's generations radiates from each page. Each book in the Leora Series is a stand-alone. Their connective threads bind them together.

Leora Goff Wilson instinctively knew that her saving of letters, photographs, memorabilia with her journaling would hold special meaning in a future that had not yet crystalized. She would undoubtedly be proud, albeit a little humbled, at how her treasures inspired her granddaughter Joy to reimagine their tellings for new generations. Dive into these pages and experience adventures akin to *Little House on the Prairie* meets *Our Town*.

—**John Busbee**, Founder of *The Culture Buzz*, Iowa Governor's Award for Partnership & Collaboration in the Arts, Iowa History Award for "Last Measure of Full Devotion," *Iowa History Journal*, also a contributor to *Our American Stories*

While I am not related to the author of *Leora's Early Years*, I feel like a long-lost cousin after reading her books. Especially in this latest book, Joy Kidney's weaving of her families' stories into a colorful tapestry that can help the reader appreciate their own families' stories. *Leora's Early Years* is a heartwarming narrative of real people who lived real lives in real places that we can find on a map. We of the 21st century have much to learn from the lives of Joy's family of the 19th and early-20th centuries.

—**Arvid Huisman**, former newspaper publisher, regular columnist for *Iowa History Journal*, as well as several newspapers, author of *More Country Roads*

So often, the histories of Iowa's rural families are reduced to names and dates on tombstones, or simple facts listed in family genealogies, if they are preserved at all. Joy Neal Kidney has given us a gift with this remarkable book that shares the joys, heartbreaks and hopes of her Iowa ancestors as they built a life in Guthrie County and beyond. It takes a tremendous amount of research, time and skill to tell these stories in a way that will resonate today. Joy has accomplished this. Using the history of her family, she humanizes a pivotal era of Iowa history, when the horse-and-buggy days of the late 1800s gave way to the early twentieth century, an era filled with technological marvels and optimism for a brighter future.

Even if you've never attended a country school, lived on a farm or had an escapade at a jail (don't miss that story!), you can relate to being a kid, enjoying the company of family and friends, losing a loved one, and experiencing simple pleasures in life, like music, fairs and holidays. While these stories will entertain you, they also honor the things that really matter in life—family, faith, service to community and country, resilience, and leaving a legacy of a life well lived.

—**Darcy Maulsby**, MBA, 5th generation farmer, Iowa's Storyteller, author of several books, including *Madison County* and *A Culinary History of Iowa*

Joy Neal Kidney, known as the 'keeper' of her family's history, has done another masterful job of sharing that history with interested readers. Working in reverse chronological order, she began telling the family saga with *Leora's Letters: The Story of Love and Loss for an Iowa Family During World War II*, continued it with *Leora's Dexter Stories: The Scarcity Years of the Great Depression*, and now has reached even farther back to pioneering days with *Leora's Early Years*. The included map, family tree, and numerous photos and newspaper articles add to the narrative. After one reads the entire series, he or she will almost feel as though the subjects are known as well as members of one's own family. It certainly will give readers a greater appreciation for his or her own family's history and inspire them to begin preserving it for future generations. Kidney is certainly doing an admirable job of obeying the biblical command to 'honor thy father and thy mother.'

> —**Dennis L. Peterson**, historian, author of several books, including *Look Unto the Hills: Stories of Growing Up in Rural East Tennessee*, and a regular contributor to *Our American Stories*

Author Joy Neal Kidney's latest account of her family's struggles and triumphs in the lean years of pioneer Iowa is as informative as it is inviting. *Leora's Early Years* highlights her ability to weave these exploits into readable and relatable stories, and makes excellent use of her access to her family's detailed documentation, the completeness of which is nearly unprecedented. Barring living through such times yourself, I believe that *Leora's Early Years* represents the truest account of life in Iowa in that era, and may serve as a catalyst in the research and preservation of one's own family stories. In any regard, *Leora's Early Years* certainly will warm the heart, tug at the emotions, and deepen the respect of all those readers who have pioneer ancestors in their family trees.

> —**Mark A. Peitzman**, Historian and Preservationist, formerly with the State Historical Society of Iowa (SHSI) and the Iowa Dept. of Cultural Affairs (DCA)

The oldest of ten children, Leora Goff grew up mostly on farms in Guthrie County, but she was not allowed to attend high school. Her folks, both with Iowa pioneer ancestors, relied on her sturdy and cheerful help with everything from childcare to chickens, cooking and canning to washing and ironing, gardening to fieldwork. Leora developed the tenacity, optimism, and hope she'd need to endure three brothers drafted for the Great War, the loss of family members, and marriage to Clabe Wilson. Clabe's alcoholic father had died, leaving his unstable mother with two small children. These undercurrents forged Clabe and Leora into the parents they'd need to become to successfully shepherd their family through two great eras of world and local history—the Great Depression and WWII.

—**Rod Stanley**, historian, speaker, Guthrie County
Historical Village and Museum Board, Dexter Museum
Board, who has also contributed to *Our American Stories*

Leora's Early Years

GUTHRIE COUNTY ROOTS

JOY NEAL KIDNEY

Published by Legacy Press
Your life tells a story; we can help you write it.
Legacypress.org

For permission, please write to joynealkidney@gmail.com

Printed in the United States of America

Library of Congress Control Number:

ISBN (softcover): 978-1-7341587-4-8
ISBN (hardcover): 978-1-7341587-8-6
ISBN (ebook): 978-1-7341587-5-5

Available from Amazon.com and other retail outlets

"Morrisburg Cemetery" Copyright © 2014, 2022 by Nicholas Dowd

Cover and interior design and layout by Nelly Murariu @PixBeeDesign.com

Author photo by Emina Hastings

For Kate

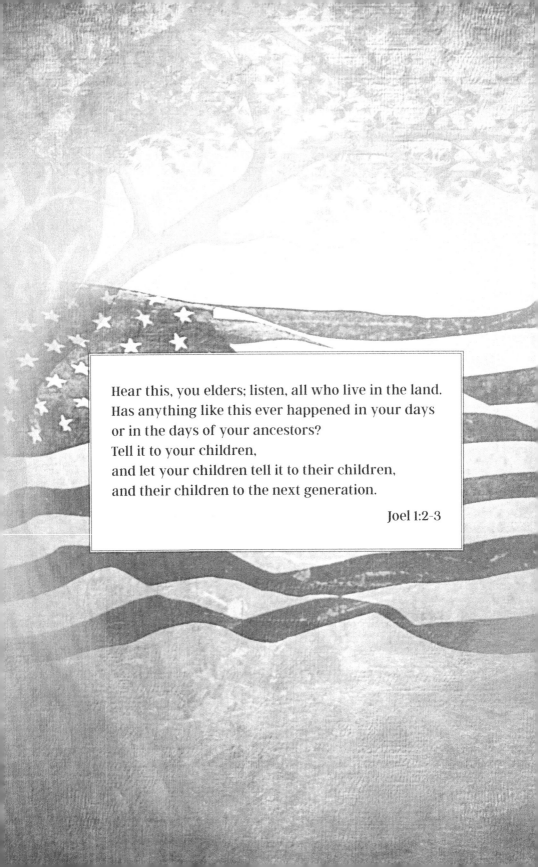

Hear this, you elders; listen, all who live in the land.
Has anything like this ever happened in your days
or in the days of your ancestors?
Tell it to your children,
and let your children tell it to their children,
and their children to the next generation.

Joel 1:2-3

Table of Contents

Foreword

by Lee Habeeb

To start any tribute to a storyteller, or a terrific book filled with great stories—which Joy Neal Kidney's *Leora's Early Years* most certainly is—it is always best to begin with the great Greek philosopher Plato, who understood a thing or two about the world all those thousands of years ago. "Those who tell the stories, rule society," Plato said.

Stories also shape society. They shape who we are. And who we're to become. That perennial best-seller The Bible—the most important book ever written, and the biggest best-seller of all time—is nothing but an endless series of stories: Adam and Eve. Cain and Abel. The Prodigal Son. And it is filled with some remarkable characters: Noah, Abraham, Jacob, Joseph, Leah, Esther, Sarah—and two women named Mary.

What's so powerful about the Bible is that human beings across the globe have been stepping into those stories for centuries into the lives of those characters—and seeing themselves in them.

Poet Muriel Rukeyser famously said this: "The world is made up of stories, not atoms." Those words are true. Storytelling is indeed the world's best—and oldest—killer App.

In his last address to the nation in 1989 from the Oval Office, President Ronald Reagan spoke about the importance of storytelling, too. He talked about the Mayflower and the Doolittle Raids and the young men who stormed the beaches of Normandy. Then he said these words: "If we forget what we did, we will forget who we are."

FAMILY STORIES

Reagan was right. And it is why I believe the book that you are about to read is important. Because storytelling isn't just for historians with fancy degrees or professional writers looking to pen the next bestseller. It's important work for all of us. Because all of us have stories to tell about our own families—stories that started long before we were born. If we forget what our forefathers did, what our family members who came before us did, and the family that came before them, we'll forget who we are.

I first came to know Joy Neal Kidney while hosting the nationally syndicated radio show and podcast, *Our American Stories*. Each night, I routinely ask our listeners on over 200 stations nationwide to send in stories of their own. Our team then reads the submissions, and when one seems right for the show, we ask the writer to record it. Through this process, we've discovered several superb regular contributors—none finer than our friend who listens faithfully on the legendary iHeart station in Des Moines, Iowa—1040 WHO. I am lucky to now call her a friend.

Joy's storytelling manner is very much a product of her midwestern nature - straight as straight can be. And direct, too. You'll find no sentimentality in the pages that follow. And few flowery words. There will instead be many examples like this: "Laura Jordan knew that Sherd Goff was afflicted with incurable wanderlust when she married him in early 1890," the book begins. We soon learn that "their first baby, a daughter named Leora, was born in late December in snowy Guthrie County, Iowa."

That wanderlust of her father's would lead Leora and her family on adventure after adventure, including trips to other states seeking a better life. One such move—entirely based on a newspaper advertisement promising bounty of all kinds—would prompt Leora's family to settle in northeast Nebraska. To say it didn't end well would be an understatement. "Nebraska summers brought a scorching wind, blowing sand, and dust," Joy wrote of the episode. Sherd went "bust" in Nebraska and "headed back to Iowa with his family on a train."

There would be many more family moves. Some for the better, and some not. But somehow, the family not only survived those moves. That wanderlust somehow brought them closer together.

RICH CHARACTERS

There are stories short and long in this terrific book as Joy creates a landscape filled with rich characters from her family clan. Of being born with a "pioneer spirit," Joy is no reductionist. "Being born of pioneer stock doesn't guarantee a darn thing," she writes. "Not when you're born to a farmer in Guthrie County, Iowa. Not when your farmer father yearns for greener pastures. Not with drought, with a war and a pandemic in the future. But Leora's ancestors had great hopes when they traveled on horseback and in wagons, across miles of prairie, to a new state."

Always, Joy reminds us that life isn't what it used to be. And that there was a time when life was in many ways much harder. But in other ways, much easier. And in some ways better. "The Goffs had no phone, no home mail delivery, so they never knew when someone might drop by," Joy writes in the pages to come. "But they had plenty of meat and vegetables which had been put up in Mason jars or stored in a root cellar. Mamma could quickly put together a meal of chicken and noodles, Leora remembered. She'd send a child to catch the chicken, which was easy if their dog was trained to help."

One chapter, entitled "Decoration Day 1900," is filled with images that draw readers back in time to the streets she describes: "Nine-year-old Leora was one of about twenty young girls who took part in a solemn ceremony. Civil War and Spanish American War veterans decorated a hayrack wagon, which was pulled to the Guthrie Center cemetery by a team of Palomino horses.

The young girls, dressed in white—with red, white, and blue sashes over their shoulders—rode on the wagon. The veterans marched behind."

Joy also writes about prior eras without judgment, as it is not helpful to judge people outside of their times and context. "Leora had hoped to continue in high school, but Pa declared that as the oldest of ten children, she was needed on the farm to help feed them all, help with the laundry, and help with the younger ones."

Sometimes, even short sentences—this one describing the 1909 Iowa State Fair - remind readers of how things have changed in the world. "Wireless telegraphing flashed messages across the Fairgrounds and motorcycle races were held for the first time. Iowa women rallied there for the right to vote."

WEDDING

There's even a lovely paragraph in which Joy describes how Leora's husband proposed. As for the wedding, Joy's description is both brief and humorous.

"Clabe Wilson and Leora Goff were married in the Goff home near Wichita February 15, 1914," Kidney writes. "The noon wedding was late because the minister, John Carl Orth from Guthrie Center, had a difficult time getting through the eight miles of snow drifts with his team and buggy."

The family would live through the Spanish flu—a global pandemic that killed nearly 20 million people. Over 500,000 of those deaths were Americans. Over 6,500 were Iowans. Leora and her family would survive smallpox, witness a social revolution as women won the right to vote, and have loved ones serve in not one but two World Wars.

And through it all, Leora knew the value of love. Family. And God. And—of course—work. Always and everywhere, there was work to be done.

She sold chickens and eggs, which enabled the mother of seven to buy a new Singer sewing machine through the Sears catalog—the Amazon of its day.

There was little Leora didn't do for her family. And she did it all in what may well be the most remarkable century to have ever lived.

Thanks to Joy Neal Kidney, I feel like I now know a remarkable, strong woman, and a big, beautiful family. I know a lot more about life in the late 19th and early 20th century. And a lot more about Iowa and America, too.

Here's hoping her writing inspires all of us to do the same for our families. For our communities. And our country.

—**Lee Habeeb** is the founder and host of *Our American Stories*, a talk radio executive, and *Newsweek* essayist. He is a University of Virginia Law School graduate and lives in beautiful Oxford, Mississippi with his wife Valerie, daughter Reagan, two pugs (Leroy Jenkins and Bubba), two cats (Spunky and Mario) and twelve chickens.

Morrisburg Cemetery

"For all flesh is as grass, and all the glory
of man as the flower of the grass. The
grass withereth, and flower thereof
falleth away. But the word of the Lord
endureth forever. . ." I Peter 1:24-25

At the edge
Of the Stuart Road
Sleep the Morrisburg souls.
A hilltop town
Flourishing for a time,
Before splintering
In a storm.
Without warning
Their time came.
Now years of serenity
Cover them
On this high curve.
Decades of summers
Shelter these souls.
A community of friends
Stilled, and now settled
Patiently at rest,
Men, women, children
awaiting the archangel call.
He will find them all
Here, south of Panora
Amid the tallgrass drifts.

—Nicholas Dowd (2014)

1920s Guthrie County map

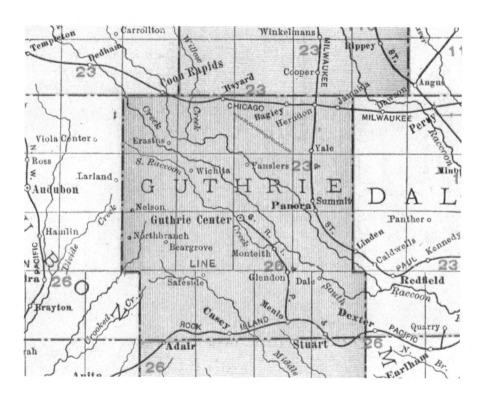

Goff Family Members

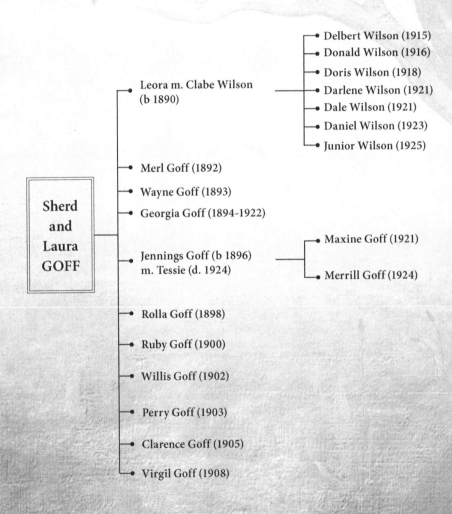

Sherd and Laura GOFF

- Leora m. Clabe Wilson (b 1890)
  - Delbert Wilson (1915)
  - Donald Wilson (1916)
  - Doris Wilson (1918)
  - Darlene Wilson (1921)
  - Dale Wilson (1921)
  - Daniel Wilson (1923)
  - Junior Wilson (1925)
- Merl Goff (1892)
- Wayne Goff (1893)
- Georgia Goff (1894-1922)
- Jennings Goff (b 1896) m. Tessie (d. 1924)
  - Maxine Goff (1921)
  - Merrill Goff (1924)
- Rolla Goff (1898)
- Ruby Goff (1900)
- Willis Goff (1902)
- Perry Goff (1903)
- Clarence Goff (1905)
- Virgil Goff (1908)

CHAPTER 1

Land of the Santee Sioux (1892)

Laura Jordan knew that Sherd Goff was afflicted with incurable wanderlust when she married him in early 1890. They both grew up in Iowa, but she assured him she could live anywhere as long as it was part of the United States and was near a school where their youngsters could attend.

Milton Sheridan "Sherd" Goff and Laura Arminta Jordan

Their first baby, a daughter named Leora, was born in late December in snowy Guthrie County, Iowa. Just over a year later, first son Merl joined the family.

Soon Sherd decided he wanted to find a better place to live. An extensive and widely circulated newspaper article from neighboring Nebraska touted Bloomfield as a wonderful new community. The *Bloomfield Monitor* advertised beautiful and fertile land for sale, with businesses already begun. With other Guthrie County men, Sherd traveled to northeast Nebraska, taking the railroad as far as the tracks took them. Some decided to sell out and move there.

"It don't look like much now." When he got back, he spread the newspaper on the table. "It says here that 'Knox County is favored with sunshine and showers, mild winters and grand growing summers where the failure of crops has been unknown. The best country on earth.'

"I think we can really make a go of it in Nebraska. What do you think, Laura?"

Zenas and Emma Barnes, Sherd's Guthrie County cousins, moved right away. So Laura would already know folks there.

"What about schools? I want the children to be able to go to school." Wearing a long cotton housedress protected by an apron, Laura patted baby Merl, who snuggled against her shoulder.

"It says here that Bloomfield has built a $5000 school and they're already holding classes."

"What about Indians? Aren't they the ones sent to Nebraska after killing those people in Minnesota?"

"Laura, that happened before the Civil War, before you and I were even born. They are peaceful now."

"Well, Sherd, whatever you think best."

He sold their cows and chickens, their beds and the cookstove, the table and chairs. They packed their clothes in trunks and wooden boxes, and dressed in their best clothes to board the train, probably at the Guthrie Center depot. Bloomfield—about 200 miles west—was the end of the Chicago-St. Paul-Minneapolis and Omaha line in northeast Nebraska.

"Homes for the homeless, land for the landless," Sherd quoted from the newspaper. "That's us. I believe Nebraska will grow good crops for us."

Pregnant again, Laura, Sherd, and their two small children crossed the Missouri River to the new town, founded just three years earlier. Leora was two years old, and Merl just a year old when they moved, probably in late 1892. They likely stayed with cousins Zenas and Emma Barnes until they could get their own start.

Wayne Goff was born there February 24, 1893.

Wayne, Leora, and Merl Goff, 1893, Hartington, Nebraska

Leora and Merl ran barefoot in the sand and enjoyed watching prairie dogs chase from mound to mound. When it did rain, goldenrod and other wildflowers bloomed on the prairie. Coyotes howled at night. Mourning doves cooed softly, redwing blackbirds shrieked as they perched on waving cattails.

Nebraska summers brought a scorching wind, blowing sand and dust. To the chorus tune of "Beulah Land," Laura, in her sweet alto voice, sang "Ah, Nebraska land, sweet Nebraska land, upon thy burning soil I stand, and I look away, across the plains, and I wonder why it never rains."

Sherd reminded her of what the newspaper had said. "Every summer can't be hot and dry. We'll eventually have a bumper crop. You'll see."

The next spring, Georgia Laurayne Goff was born. Little Leora's first memory was of a woman holding the baby sister for the children to see. That was April 29, 1894.

The summer of 1895, Leora begged her father to let her ride a horse. When he saw how well the four-year-old took to the gentle horse, he allowed her to ride bareback after the cows in the pasture. But she slid off when the horse came to a rise. She cried, but wasn't hurt. Only her pride, she wrote decades later.

Kem Luther, in *Cottonwood Roots*, said that Nebraska home-steaders knew there was "a line out there where the rain ended... We know today that this line twists its way through the heart of Nebraska like a rattlesnake. . .. But when the droughts of the nineties came it was clear that the snaking line was a sidewinder, and that the line of rainfall could shift unpredictably eastward to lands bordering the Missouri River."

This sidewinder was closing in on Knox County, Nebraska.

CHAPTER 2

Indians Visit

"Leora, please check on the baby, then help the boys wash up." Merl and Wayne were about four and two years old.

Mamma, hair pinned up and sleeves rolled to her elbows, wearing an apron over her long dress, set out bowls and spoons for midday dinner. She returned to the hot black stove, where she cooked even in summer.

Leora, nearly five years old and wearing a dress, saw that the baby was still sleeping. She started for the door. Shadowy figures stood just inside.

Indians.

"Mamma." Though Leora's heart beat faster, she spoke quietly. Mamma turned from the stove holding a large spoon.

The Goffs were used to the sound of hoofbeats to signal someone arriving, or at least a knock at the door. But the Indians had approached silently, as was their custom, and quietly entered a house without knocking. Mamma never got used to it. The Indians didn't come often but they always startled her.

Pa said they wouldn't hurt them but Leora knew her mother was uneasy when Indians slipped silently into the house when Pa wasn't home.

Three men dressed in pants and shirts, just like Sherd and the other settlers. One had long black hair and wore moccasins, but the others wore boots just like Pa. They carried folds of cloth, which meant they wanted to barter for something, probably chickens.

"Go ahead and get your brothers," Mamma told Leora.

"Those Indians?" Wayne asked his big sister.

"Hush. Yes, they're Indians."

"I told ya." Merl puffed out his chest.

Leora dipped a little water from the barrel into a pan on a wooden table outside. "We're supposed to wash up for dinner." Merl washed his hands while Leora helped with Wayne's grubby ones. All three children were barefoot.

"Tiptoe in and sit at the table."

"Aren't you afraid?"

"Whisper." She shooed them inside.

Leora helped Wayne onto a chair. The men had unfolded a little of the fabric—dark prints of blue and red cotton. One man pointed outside to a nearby pen of chickens.

Three pairs of eyes watched Mamma and the Indians.

Baby Georgia began to whimper. Leora slipped off her chair to gather her little sister from the cradle. She stood rocking from foot to foot, soothing the baby while watching her mother motion with her hand how much of the blue fabric she was willing to trade for.

"Leora, please go out and catch a hen." Leora handed the baby to her mother on her way out to the dusty chicken area. She grabbed the wire hook by the pen, deftly caught a hen by the leg, and lugged it upside down by the feet to the doorway. Mamma motioned to hand it to one of the men.

He turned to Mamma, holding up two fingers, then pointing to the hen. She paused a second during the transaction, then nodded yes. Leora soon caught another one, shyly glancing up at the man's dark eyes as she held it out to him.

Leora took the baby again while her mother found the scissors kept high in a cupboard. She smoothed the Indigo blue fabric and carefully cut across it. She folded it while the men carried the remaining fabric and the chickens outside.

"Hee-haw, hee-haw." Pa's mules had come up to the gate. The visitors laughed, gesturing to each other about the mules' long ears, then left as quietly as they'd arrived.

Leora giggled behind a sun-browned hand, her speckled brown eyes shining. "Wait 'til Pa finds out the Indians made fun of his mules."

Mamma began to spoon stew onto their dishes. "Wait 'til Pa finds out how brave you were."

CHAPTER 3

Drought and Dust Storms

After the Sioux uprisings in Minnesota, the Santee Sioux had been ordered to settle in Knox County, in the area of Nebraska that didn't grow crops very well—unless they got plenty of rain. The government divided out land for them, men from the Indian Agency taught them to grow crops like the settlers, and missionaries built schools and taught them about the Bible.

For Sioux men, trained as hunters and warriors, fieldwork was women's work. They soon figured out how to work less and earn more by renting their lands to the white settlers. Instead of farming, they traded dress goods and other items to the settlers for cash or chickens.

The Santee in the area didn't wear paint and feathers, and didn't live in teepees either. They lived in small houses just like everyone else.

January 4, 1896, Utah became the 45th state in the union. On that same date, Leora Goff got a special angel note from her teacher, Nelly Foley, for "not whispering."

Nebraska seemed to bring drought every summer, school in the fall and spring, and a new baby Goff every winter. In early 1896, Jennings Bryan Goff was born, named for the Nebraska newspaperman and orator, William Jennings Bryan, whom Sherd greatly admired.

That summer brought more hot, dry wind and dust storms. The Goffs didn't know it then, but that area of the prairie was in a ten-year cycle of drought. Those hopeful families from Iowa had moved there at the worst possible time. The coarse grass crackled and hurt Leora's bare feet. Sandburs skittered over the dust. And prairie fires were always a threat. Where would they get water if they had a fire? One never came near, but a foreboding glow on the horizon usually meant smoke would drift to their home.

As the burdens proved too heavy, Sherd and Laura Goff were forced to sell out and move into the town of Bloomfield, which had been founded just two months before Leora was born. Sherd bought a hardware store and ran a horse-drawn delivery wagon. But when the crops failed, settlers couldn't pay their bills in town for the things they'd charged at his store.

A June newspaper announced a sheriff's sale for land belonging to M.S. and Laura Goff, their hopes turned into dust. During the worst decade to try to make a go of it in Knox County, Nebraska, drought was an unwelcome settler.

Unfortunately, Sherd went "bust" in Nebraska. His land was appraised and offered "for sale to the highest bidder for cash in hand," at 10:00 a.m. July 31, 1896, at the front door of the Grand Army of the Republic hall, in Niobrara, Nebraska.

The *Bloomfield Monitor* noted other foreclosures. Even the Bloomfield State Bank went belly up.

The Goff family—Sherd and Laura, Leora, Merl, Wayne, Georgia, and baby Jennings—headed back to Iowa on the train. Sherd tried to make it an adventure, encouraging his youngsters to look out the windows. "We're about to leave Nebraska. Now, watch for the big muddy Missouri River."

The train's iron wheels clicked and clacked on the rails, rocking their seats from side to side, the scenery rushing by. Leora was fascinated by the swirling murkiness of the big river.

"When we get to the other side, we'll be back in Iowa." They could see the green shore of Iowa ahead.

"I'll be glad to see Grandpap and Grandmother again." Leora sat next to little Georgia.

"We still have a ways to go, but Grandpap will be waiting for us at the depot with his wagon." Mamma held baby Jennings, who'd slept most of the ride.

Sherd kept an eye on Wayne and Merl. "We'll start over again at home, and at least there won't be any Indians to make Mamma nervous."

June 25, 1896, The Bloomfield Monitor

CHAPTER 4

Pioneer Stock (1850s)

Being born of pioneer stock doesn't guarantee a darn thing. Not when you're born to a farmer in Guthrie County, Iowa. Not when your farmer father yearns for greener pastures. Not with a drought, or a war, or a pandemic in the future.

But Leora's folks came from sturdy family roots, stretching back to eastern states, and swept up in part of the nation's nineteenth century's westward expansion.

Iowa had become the 29th State in the Union in 1846, the same year Neptune was discovered. It was also the year a baby girl was born to Ephraim and Lucy Jane (Branson) Moore in Indiana. They named their sixth child Emelia Ann. Emelia would become Leora Goff's beloved grandmother. In Iowa.

Leora's grandparents carried great hopes with them as they traveled on horseback and in wagons, across miles of prairie, to a new state.

In 1846 as well, Sam Wilson (who grew up with Indians in Ohio) married Emily Huyck in Illinois. They became grandparents of Clabe Wilson. In Iowa.

Decades later, Leora Goff married Clabe Wilson, both Iowa born.

Following are short sketches of Leora's and Clabe's pioneer ancestries and their growing up years.

1850s

CLABE'S ANCESTORS:
THE WILSONS AND THE WILLIAMSES

In 1854, Sam and Emily Wilson, whose son Daniel would become Clabe Wilson's father, were early settlers in Guthrie and Carroll County, Iowa.

John and Harriett Williams pioneered in Guthrie County in 1854, "when the wilderness was a mass of howling savage beasts, and smoky wigwams of the dusky savage warrior were the only occupants," according to his obituary.

The next year, their son Samuel Williams and his wife Martha arrived in Iowa from Ohio. Their youngest daughter, Georgia, became the mother of Clabe Wilson.

In 1855, when Franklin Pierce was President of the United States, there were no railroads yet west of the Mississippi River. The wagons of these early pioneers crossed the mighty Mississippi by ferry to reach their new state.

Martha (Barr or Bower) and Samuel Williams

LEORA'S ANCESTORS: THE MOORES

When Emelia Ann Moore was eight years old, her family loaded two wagons in Indiana. Starting out on May 6, 1855, Ephraim and Lucy Moore, along with six children, began their historic trek across Indiana and Illinois. They arrived in Guthrie County on June 2 and moved in with Emelia's Uncle John Branson's family for two months. By then, Ephraim had obtained a patent on a farm on Beaver Creek, six miles south of Guthrie Center.

Indians often visited the pioneers in those verdant hills. Ephraim Moore was a farmer, carpenter, schoolteacher, and Baptist minister. Six more children were born to Lucy and Ephraim. Three of those died young and are among the many early graves under the ancient pines in the Monteith cemetery.

The original farm remained in his possession as long as he lived. His great granddaughter, Leora, would live there twice—once as a child, then as a married woman.

Ephraim W. and Lucy Jane (Branson) Moore

When Emelia Ann Moore grew up, she married David Jordan. Their firstborn was Laura, the mother of our Leora.

CHAPTER 5

Leora's Grandparents: The Jordans (1860s)

These Jordans were latecomers to Guthrie County. After his mother had died, David Jordan, age 23, arrived from Ohio in 1865 with his father Elijah. David, a rural businessman and preacher (Church of Jesus Called Sharon of Regular Predestinarian Baptists, according to his obituary), married Emelia Moore. Their first child was born in their log cabin in 1868 a half mile east of Monteith. They named her Laura Arminta, and she would become Leora's mother.

David and Emelia Ann (Moore) Jordan

By this time, not long after the end of the Civil War, the nation had 31 states, recently adding Nebraska.

Laura's next three siblings died while still youngsters. When Laura was eight years old, a sister was born who grew to adulthood with her, along with five more Jordan children.

THE GOFFS

Nathan P. Goff migrated to Iowa from Indiana during the Civil War, 1863. He legally paid for a substitute so that his son, John B. Goff, could avoid the draft. The family settled near Fairview in Madison County where, according to family history, the first crop of corn that Nathan Goff planted in Iowa was with the help of two of his daughters, one sitting on each side of his planter, dropping the seed as he drove a team of mules.

Nathan P. and Elizabeth (Norris) Goff

Nathan and Elizabeth's son, John B. Goff, married Florence Shepherd in 1864. The next year they became parents of Milton Sheridan "Sherd" Goff, whose firstborn was our Leora.

John Broderick and Florence (Shepherd) Goff

CLABE'S PARENTS:
THE WILSONS AND THE WILLIAMSES

During that same decade, twins Daniel Ross and George Wilson were born in 1868 near Coon Rapids. Only Daniel would survive.

Georgia Ann Williams, born near Dale City in 1864, married Frank Davis when she was 17. They had a son Fred before divorcing. A few years later, Georgia married Daniel Ross Wilson, who didn't want her son living with them, so Fred grew up with his grandparents, Sam and Martha Williams.

Dan and Georgia Wilson's firstborn was Claiborne Daniel Wilson, born in 1888, called Clabe.

CHAPTER 6

Leora Goff is Born (1890)

Oklahoma Territory was created in 1890. Idaho and Wyoming became states. Yosemite was named a National Park. The town of Bloomfield, Nebraska, was founded. Laura Jordan married "Sherd" Goff. And Leora Goff was born.

Three years earlier, Laura Jordan began teaching at a country school in Guthrie County. A watch was a must for a school teacher, so Laura bought one, a gold Elgin with flowers engraved on the case, front and back.

But in those days, when a woman married, she could no longer teach school. Laura needed a cow more than the watch. David Jordan made a deal with his oldest daughter—a cow for the watch. So Laura's mother Emelia wore it instead.

One of Laura's friends was Minnie Belle Goff, who taught in a rural school. She was the only sister of Sherd Goff, and that was probably how Laura met Sherd.

They were married in February 1890. That September, Laura's mother Emelia, whose youngest child Fred Jordan was just a year old, gave her daughter a New Testament. "Presented by her Mother Sept. 30, 1890."

On December 4, Laura's first baby was born. Leora Frances Goff was also the first grandchild for both sides of the family.

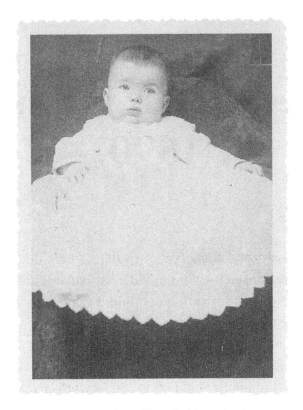

Leora Francis Goff, probably early 1891

Leora was still a baby when more tragedy befell Sherd Goff's parents. Of the seven children born to them, only three survived to age 20. The youngest sons had died before the age of four. That left the four oldest: Sherd, Edwin (who never married), Henry, and Minnie.

The Christmas before Sherd and Laura married, an overheated Henry Goff rode his horse home after attending a dance. He died of pneumonia on December 30, 1889. Henry Goff was 20.

Then on May Day of 1892, a rainy Sunday. Minnie Goff boarded with a family during the school week, then spent weekends at home with her folks. Minnie's beau picked her up at home with a team of horses and a buggy to return to where she boarded during the school week. They encountered flooding at Patterson's ford and a deluge washed them down South Beaver Creek. Two men found a buggy cushion in a drift on the creek bank, along with a lady's handbag. Downstream they located the young man's body.

Farther down, the lifeless young teacher lay against the opposite muddy bank. Minnie was 20. The men discovered the buggy and the team—one horse still alive, just its head sticking out of the stream.

That left only Sherd and Ed of the seven Goff siblings. Minnie, their only sister, had been Laura's friend.

Sherd's own family grew when their first son, Emery Merl, was born earlier that year. In January 1892. They called him by his middle name, Merl.

CHAPTER 7

Iowa Again (1896)

When the Goffs returned to Guthrie County the spring of 1896, cardinal songs welcomed them, along with woodpeckers and migrating geese. Pale green thickets lined the country roads. Sprouting oak leaves were the size of the ears of baby squirrels.

At Grandpap Jordan's farm, Leora's aunts, Floy and Lottie, ages 20 and 18, ran out to welcome the family. When they unbuttoned Leora's coat to see what she had on, it was the same old dress she wore when they'd moved to Nebraska. But they were delighted with having five nieces and nephews to dote on.

Leora started first grade that September in the nice-sized town of Stuart. With a population of 2,000, Stuart still had dirt streets and boardwalks on the main street, and hitching rails for horses. Leora's teacher was Elizabeth Myers.

Early Stuart, showing the dirt street, boardwalks, and hitching rails

Girls wore their hair long in those days but when Leora came down with the whooping cough, she ran a fever. Her head was so tender and her dark hair began falling out. Stuart's lady doctor told Laura that she should cut her daughter's hair short.

Incumbent Democratic President, Grover Cleveland, did not run for office that year. The Nebraska politician, William Jennings Bryan, was nominated on the Democratic ticket. Sherd Goff certainly approved. He brought home folded paper Bryan caps for his three older youngsters to wear to school.

But William McKinley, former Governor of Ohio, was elected president, the last to have served in the Civil War.

The day before Christmas, Sherd did a little shopping in downtown Stuart. When he got home he said he met Santa Claus who gave him their presents. How nice of Santa, and the kids got to open them on Christmas eve.

The next morning the excited family rose early to prepare for Christmas at Grandpap Jordan's, just west of Monteith. For special occasions, the youngsters were allowed in the parlor, a sort of hallowed place, Leora remembered many decades later. The legs of the parlor stand ended in claws holding glass balls. A hanging lamp, painted with roses and with glass spangles dripping from the edges, lit the big dining room table. Grandmother's treasures included a vinegar cruet and a poppy plate.

It was good to be back home in Iowa with so many aunts and uncles and grandparents.

1897

Home of David and Emelia Jordan ½ mile west of Monteith, Iowa, 1897.
L-R: David and Emelia (Moore) Jordan, Fred Jordan (their youngest),
Laura (Jordan) Goff (their oldest) with Georgia Goff in front,
Floy (Jordan) Cowden with Jennings Goff in front, Millie Crawley (friend),
Lottie (Jordan) Anderson, Cora Jordan with Leora Goff in front,
Herb Cowden with Wayne Goff in front, M. S. "Sherd" Goff
with Merl Goff in front.

CHAPTER 8

Robinson Circus (1898)

Sherd was a hard-working man, but he was also a fan of the circus, fairs, or of any celebration. Louis Cyr, the Strongest Man in the World, came to Guthrie Center with the Robinson Circus in September 1898. It's likely that Sherd took his older kids to see this one.

"Father always liked the circus," Leora wrote decades later. "I don't think we ever missed going when the circus came to town and there were several small circuses that came to small towns then. I remember someone saying to Pa, 'Well, you came to town to see the circus?' 'Yes,' Pa said, 'I had to bring the kids.' He was as much a kid as we were."

From the poster: "**Circus day will be inaugurated with a brilliant street parade, which will leave the show grounds promptly at ten o'clock and traverse the principal downtown streets.**"

Pa and the kids probably arrived before ten o'clock to watch the parade. Maybe a younger brother or two of Mamma's rode along in the wagon—the Jordan boys: Floyd (18), Collis (15), and even Fred (9); plus Sherd's own older youngsters—Leora (7), Merl (6), Wayne (5), and perhaps even Georgia (4), since Leora could watch out for her. Grandpap, father of the Jordan boys, enjoyed having fun with his grandchildren, so I imagine he was with them.

The Guthrian, September 15, 1898

Watch for Circus Day.
Everybody Enthusiastic Over Coming of
the Big Robinson Show.

"The ... famous John Robinson Greatest of All American Shows [coming] to Guthrie Center Wednesday September 21 has aroused wide spread interest, and it is safe to predict that the show will receive an enthusiastic public welcome. No show that has ever exhibited here has ever been preceded by a more flattering reputation. The unusual merit of this great show is known and appreciated, and it is doubtful whether any other similar exhibition could so thorough arouse the show going public, and create the same degree of anticipatory enthusiasm."

The John Robinson Show had joined The Ringling Brothers earlier that year. Twenty-two railcars plus 2 advance cars of Robinson property plus Ringling animals and equipment. The show included six elephants and one hippo, with 14 cages of animals. The Robinson show opened April 27 in Baraboo, Wisconsin, that year, then toured Wisconsin and Iowa. This circus even stopped in the town of Guthrie Center, with a population then of just over 1000 citizens.

Louis Cyr, the strongest man in the world

"The show has been so thoroughly heralded that it would be difficult to add anything new in the way of announcement, and attention can simply be called again to the paramount features of the great exhibition, which include Louis Cyr, the strongest man in the world; the Harvey Family, of bicyclists; Samuel Burt, whose feats of equilibrium on the independent ladder are simply marvelous; William Dutton, Julie Lowande, and a dozen other famous lady and gentleman riders, and a long list of novel attractions to be seen only with this magnificent exhibition."

With baby Rolla just one week old, Mamma probably stayed home with two-year-old Jennings. Her own mother may have come for the day, along with her sisters Floy, age 23 and not married yet, and twelve-year-old Cora.

THE JOHN ROBINSON GREATEST
OF ALL AMERICAN SHOWS

"The John Robinson menagerie, with its mammoth hippopotamus and scores of dens of rare wild beasts, is without an equal in the United States, and the hippodrome races are rendered thrillingly realistic by the introduction of the finest Kentucky and Arabian horses."

At one time, Sherd hoped to travel and work for a circus. He could do handstands in the house and even a complete flip, outside, for his kids. They all tried to do his tricks as well.

> **"Every Morning at 10 O'clock, Rain or Shine, the Most Resplendent Free Street Parade Ever Witnessed, Millions Expended in this Dazzling Display, Gratuitously Offered to the Public. Two Performances Daily, Afternoon at 2, Night at 8. Doors Open One Hour Earlier. One 50 Cent Ticket Admits to All. Children, Under 12 Years, Half Price."**

What an exciting day for rural families who flocked into Guthrie Center. They'd take time off from fieldwork, probably do a little shopping while they were in town, and bring home memories of rousing exhibits. Who would want to miss the most resplendent free street parade to come to Guthrie Center? And thrilling hippodrome races? Or a glimpse of the strongest man in the world?

CHAPTER 9

Prairie College School, First "Talking Machine"

The Goff family lived east of Monteith for a while, then moved to the pioneer farm of Ephraim Moore, south of Guthrie Center, along what is now Highway 25. The older Goff youngsters walked to rural Prairie College country school along a dirt road, carrying their dinner pails.

These days you can tell where a one-room school used to stand, on the corner of two rural roads, by old-fashioned orange lilies lining the road. Did pioneers bring those lilies with them to Iowa?

Those prolific flowers aren't native, they aren't wild, they aren't even real lilies. They are daylilies, from the genus Hemerocallis, which are native to China, Japan, and Korea. Growing from a mass of roots that hold moisture and nutrients, these plants can survive for weeks out of the ground. That's how they became popular as world travelers.

Prairie College School, about 1898, 6 miles south of Guthrie Center. Eighteen children from seven families, most of them barefoot. L-R: Back: Millie Moore, Forest Crawley, Mable France, Mattie Eweing, Bessie Crawley, Carl Crawley, Elsie France, Ella Moore. Front: Verna Davis, Ida Moore, Isaac Moore, Lonnie Crawley, teacher Clara Davis (once a student of Laura Jordan), Guy Olmstead, Luella France, Ray Eweing, Leora Goff. Seated: Wayne Goff, Merl Goff.

Students took turns lugging water for the school from a nearby farmhouse. Before they began taking their own drinking cups, all the students used the same dipper.

Each bought a slate to work on, for arithmetic especially. When kids did their work with chalk on the slates, they made quite a racket. Leora used a double slate, with a little sponge to erase with, which was easier to keep clean than the rags most students used. Someone decided that slates were unsanitary. When they began to use tablets of paper, the schoolroom became much quieter.

The only time Leora was punished at school was at Prairie College. Verna Davis, who sat right in front of her, unbraided her hair and asked Leora to rebraid it, "in little braids right in school time." Verna tore her slate rag into strips to tie each braid, and used a piece of broken mirror to check the results. Verna giggled. The teacher, Bob Masters, said, "Verna. Leora. Get your spelling books and come up to the front. You will stand and study your spelling lessons there." Leora was humiliated.

They played "Steal Sticks" with bases, choosing sides, and trying to steal sticks from inside the other side's goal. "Ante Over" was another game—throwing a ball over the schoolhouse. When one side caught the ball, they'd run around to the other side and "tag" as many as they could, touching them with the ball.

" One Old Cat" and "Two Old Cat" was a ballgame that could be played with one batter or two. If a player was "crossed out" by throwing a homemade ball between the batter and a base, he was called out. "Follow the Leader" was quite a game, too, with several obstacles. Bats were homemade, usually from a whittled-down board, "about like an oar for the girls," Leora remembered. Boys had bats usually made from a tree limb.

During June, country roadsides bloomed with pink wild roses. The wild rose was named Iowa's State Flower that year, 1897.

It was at Prairie College that Leora first heard a talking machine, or an early radio. No one else in the family wanted to go. "Take Fanny with you," urged her father. "She will take care of you." So one summer evening, the air filled with buzzing insects, Fanny trotted along the dirt road, lined with nodding foxtails and white daisy fleabane, with Leora to the one-room school, not quite a mile away. Even though their pets were never allowed into their own house, the dog trotted right into the schoolhouse with her. Leora found a seat and Fanny curled up at her feet.

Quite a few people came to learn about this new talking machine technology. Each person's turn to listen with the earplugs seemed too short, but it was a wonderful experience, Leora later remembered.

At the end of the evening, she confidently walked home with Fanny in the moonlight.

CHAPTER 10

Horses, Chores, and the Liza Jane Train

A good dog was "rather a necessary animal on the farm," according to Leora. The Goff kids gave them names: Shep, Fanny, Sunday (named for evangelist Billy Sunday, who held revivals at Exira and Audubon), Skip, Pup, Tige (named after Buster Brown's dog in the old comics), Sport, and Snip.

A task for a couple of Goff youngsters was to drive the cows in from the pasture for milking, accompanied by the music of cowbells and mooing bovines. In the spring, Juneberries bloomed white in the nearby timber. Usually their pet dog tagged along. One dog could bring them home by itself, Leora remembered, just gently urging the cows heading for the barn.

The Goffs had no phone nor home mail delivery so they never knew when someone might drop by. But they had plenty of meat and vegetables, which had been stored in the root cellar or put up in Mason jars. Mamma could quickly put together a meal of chicken and noodles, Leora remembered. She'd send a child to catch the chicken, which was easy if their dog was trained to help.

Quickly? Mamma made her own noodles, which takes time. Someone had to dispatch that chicken, scald it, pluck off the feathers, and clean and cut it up. Leora likely helped her mother cheerfully with anything she was asked to do, even at that age.

Sherd and his father owned a threshing machine, hiring out for miles around during harvest season. The monstrous machine was powered by horses. Grandpap Goff kept the power going steadier than anyone, but he and Grandmother Goff lived in Oklahoma with their bachelor son, Ed.

Grandpap rode the train to Iowa during threshing, July or August. Sherd sent his daughters, Leora and Georgia into Guthrie Center to pick him up at the depot. Leora still wasn't quite 8 years old when she flicked the leather reins to start the team of horses and buggy the half dozen miles, with a colt following along.

Mamma watched until they were out of sight. Georgia was only four years old. The horses were reluctant to trot, so Leora stopped and climbed off to gather tall weeds to use as a whip. That seemed to do the trick.

When they got to the depot, the Liza Jane train had arrived with no grandfather. What now? Maybe he'd walked uptown. The girls drove on up to the main street. Ed Lillie, a horse trader, patted the tame colt. When it didn't follow, its mother whinnied and the colt came at a gallop. No Grandpap in town either, so the sisters rode home to clopping hoofbeats and dickcissel songs, with buzzards circling overhead.

Grandpap Goff arrived a few days later.

Leora was used to riding and driving horses. To pick up their mail at Monteith, delivered there by the Liza Jane train, Leora rode over for it. Mamma always watched for her to come over the hill on the way back.

Leora, Merl, and Wayne liked spending weekends with Grandpap and Grandmother Jordan. It was shorter to cut across the fields on foot. The kids hiked on east of Monteith to watch the Liza Jane come through "Windy Gap" on its way to drop off passengers or the mail.

The Liza Jane was the branch line of the Rock Island Railroad. From History of Menlo, Iowa: Gathering Steam for the Second Century, 1969: "The branch train, called Liza Jane or Ol' Liza, to

Guthrie Center was completed in 1880. She made two daily trips to Guthrie, carrying mail, express, and freight to Glendon, Monteith, and Guthrie. The train returned hauling hogs, cattle and grain for market. Menlo's turntable rotated Liza Jane for the second trip to Guthrie. Sometimes you could hear the engine after dark chug-chugging up the steep grade. Liza was housed at Stuart's roundhouse overnight."

At the tender ages of 6 and 7, Wayne and Merl plowed young corn. Wayne rode on the cultivator and drove the horses, while Merl handled the plow, which loosened and dug weeds from the rich black soil.

When Leora was about 6 or 7 years old, she liked to watch her father milk the cows. When she asked to try it, she did so well that it became one of her regular chores.

1898 Georgia (4), Rolla (a few months old), and Jennings Goff (2).
Georgia's short hair may have meant she'd recently had whooping cough.
That was why Leora's hair was cut short the year before.

CHAPTER 11

Winter Entertainment and Christmas

Even though farm work took up so much time, Pa found time in the winter to interact with his youngsters. He'd stand the ones of school age in a row to work on spelling words. It was practice for school "cipher" (math) and "spell down" contests after the last recess on Fridays, helping them to remember what they'd learned.

The family's water pail had ice on it those winter mornings. A heating stove took up space in the house during cold days, but the warmth was so welcome. The kids held an apple to the side of the heating stove, scorching it a little. It made a delightful aroma until their folks told them to quit.

Many folks believed that washing your hair during the winter made people more susceptible to catching colds. Instead they used a very fine comb to attempt to "clean" their hair. When Leora was old enough to care for her own hair, she washed it during the winter anyway. The family usually took baths on Saturday nights, and they all wore long underwear. Leora hated having to stuff the long legs into cotton stockings, usually black until the fad changed to tan stockings.

Mamma made suet pudding for Christmas, steaming it in a round can set in a black iron kettle. She made drop dumplings that were so light and tender, spooning the dough into chicken gravy as it bubbled.

One Christmas there was enough snow to ride to Grandpap's and Grandmother's in a bobsled. Pa readied a team of horses while the older youngsters covered the bottom of the sled with straw, then coverlets to sit on. Eager horses stamped and snorted as the family climbed in and Mamma handed out more quilts.

Starting down the lane, Pa said, "Look at the reindeer tracks! Santa was here!"

Even though they were cow tracks, the kids were delighted. Leora had hung a stocking on the back of her chair the night before. The next morning, it was on the nearby cabinet with a doll in it. Mamma explained that Santa was probably afraid it might fall from the chair.

What a good thing for Santa to think of.

CHAPTER 12

Young Clabe Wilson

Claiborne Daniel Wilson was the firstborn and only son of Daniel Ross and Georgia Ann (Williams/Davis) Wilson. He had an older stepbrother, born during his mother's brief marriage to Frank Davis.

Dan and Georgia Wilson

Dan Wilson did not want another man's son living with them, so young Fred Davis lived with Georgia's folks, Samuel and Martha Williams. Georgia, the youngest of the four Williams sisters, was a few years older than Dan Wilson.

Clabe, born in 1888, was named for a good friend of his father's, who was from the south, maybe Missouri. His twin George died at birth.

After Clabe, Georgia gave birth to two daughters, Rectha born in 1890, and Alice in 1891.

Rectha, Clabe, and Alice Wilson, 1890s

Clabe and his sisters attended rural Frog Pond School. He once said that grew up like a wolf in the timber, keeping a young wolf as a pet, which his sisters were afraid of. He rode his horse every day and almost always carried a gun.

Clabe's great grandfather Wilson had come to America from Ireland with two brothers. His son Sam was born in New York State. but the family moved to Sandusky County, Ohio, where this story takes place.

Only nine when his father died, Sam was apprenticed to a blacksmith. The smith's wife was so cruel to him that he ran away and ended up living with Indians. He grew up with them.

It wasn't uncommon for Indians to kidnap white children when one of their own died, to replace the missing one.

Sam Wilson moved with the tribe to Illinois where Chicago is now. It was only a fort then. He married an Illinois girl and they settled at Coon Rapids, Iowa. He acted as an Indian agent in Nebraska for a while, but he came back to Iowa.

Clabe heard that story as a boy. His Wilson grandparents lived just east of Coon Rapids, although grandfather Samuel Wilson died when Clabe was nine years old. Clabe became quite a hockey player and was on a local team, when the Middle Raccoon River froze over. He'd skate up the river to Coon Rapids to visit his widowed grandmother.

His Williams grandparents lived nearby, south of Panora. One time he and a friend got into trouble for riding around the Morrisburg Church, where his mother attended and which was having a revival meeting, shooting their guns in the air.

Clabe Wilson, about 1902

CHAPTER 13

Grandpap Goff Dies, Goff Reunions (1900)

OBITUARY

Nathan Poole Goff (1815-1900)

"Nathan P. Goff was born October 2d, 1815, near Wheeling, West Virginia, and died at his home in Union county, Iowa, February 23, 1900, with cancer in the mouth, age 84 years, 4 months and 21 days. From West Virginia he moved with his parents to Missouri, living there three years. He went from Missouri to Muncie, Delaware county, Indiana, and was there married to Elizabeth Norris, August 22, 1839, who died Aug. 16th, 1894. With his wife he came to Iowa in the year 1863 and settled in Madison county near Fairview, where he lived for a number of years.

"He was the father of eleven children, four sons and seven daughters, one son and one daughter preceding him in death. The others survive him, three daughters and one son are present today.

"He was converted at the age of fifteen and united with the M.E. church in West Virginia. He was one of the first members, and was the first class leader and first Sunday school superintendent of the Fairview church. A few days before his death he requested his son, Alfred. to read to him from the bible; he read the fourth chapter of 1st Thess[alonians].

"On his death bed his son asked him if he had any message for the absent children and he repeated the latter part of the 13th verse of that chapter which reads as follows: 'Concerning them which are asleep, that ye sorrow not, even as others which have no hope.'

"'For,' said he, 'I have a hope.'

"Those who have known him during his lifetime can testify to his upright character, earnest piety and strong faith in Christ. His life has been an example worthy of imitation not only by his children and relatives, but all who desire to live thorough Christian and exemplary lives in service of the Master."

These are Nathan Goff's children, the reason for the Goff reunions through the decades. Leora's letters through the Great Depression talked about enjoying the reunions. I attended some as a child.

CHAPTER 14

Decoration Day 1900

The morning of Decoration Day, nine-year-old Leora was one of about twenty young girls who took part in a solemn ceremony.

Every year May 30th was set aside especially to remember those who died in battle. Shortly after the Civil War, the commander of the Grand Army of the Republic declared it as a day "for the purpose of strewing with flowers the graves of comrades who died in defense of their country."

Ever since, towns hold commemorations for those who paid the ultimate sacrifice. That's why you'll see so many American flags in cemeteries these days, especially during the week leading up to what we now call Memorial Day.

Civil War and Spanish American War veterans in Guthrie Center decorated a hayrack wagon, which was pulled to the cemetery by a team of Palomino horses. The young girls, dressed in white—with red, white, and blue sashes over their shoulders—rode on the wagon. The veterans marched behind. At the cemetery, a girl in white accompanied a veteran in uniform to lay flowers on soldiers' graves.

According to *The Guthrian*, published the next day, "May 30th, the most sacred day to the American people, a day when all thoughts are of the things past and gone; a day of memories that soften the heart and dim the eyes; a day when a patriotic and grateful people pay tribute and render due homage to the men that by their valor, heroism and sacrifice made it possible for us to enjoy the heritage of freedom and liberty over this broad land.

"At ten o'clock A.M. the procession headed by Guthrie Center Cadets and the Military Band, followed by members of the G.A.R., civic societies, and citizens in carriages, proceeded to the cemetery where each grave of their comrades was strewn with flowers. After this ceremony was performed the procession returned to town and disbanded for dinner."

I don't know whether Leora attended the oration in the afternoon, but her father probably did. Nine-year-old Leora may have stayed home to help Mamma.

More from *The Guthrian*: "At one thirty P.M. the citizens assembled at the opera house which had been beautifully decorated to finish the ceremonies of the day. After singing by the glee club, D. Brown, the orator of the day delivered an eloquent and patriotic address, which was replete with lofty thoughts that inspired his hearers with a deeper patriotism and love of country.

Motz Opera House. The building is still standing.

"At the conclusion of his speech a flag drill was presented to a group of school girls, who in their evolutions produced a beautiful and bewildering effect. When the benediction was pronounced the memorial service of 1900 had gone into history.

"It was remarked by many that never before in Guthrie Center had there been so many in attendance, and in taking part in the ceremonies of the day. This evidence of the interest of our citizens take in observance of this day gives us assurance of the perpetuity of this day as the great day of the years."

Decades later, Leora remembered the dignified ceremony, an awe-inspiring day from her own childhood, connecting her to the nation's history.

CHAPTER 15

The Jail Escapade (1900)

Leora became involved in something risky that summer, while the family lived in town. A neighbor girl, a little older than Leora, told several youngsters about two men at the jail, which was on the grounds of the court house. She'd heard adults talking about inmates who had learned to do some craftwork while serving time in the penitentiary.

The kids were curious, so one Sunday afternoon, Gertrude Moty, Dot Ferry, Merl and Leora Goff (8, 9, and 10-year-olds) approached the jail, which had barred but open windows. Since Gertrude was the oldest, she did the talking, naming interesting items they'd heard the men could make. The prisoners said if they'd bring some pasteboard boxes and glue, they would build them something fun.

The children surreptitiously collected the materials and toted them to the jail. Visitors couldn't get near the building, so the men reached out through the bars with a broom several times to draw in the articles.

Afterwards, Leora and Merl owned up to their clandestine trips. "Never, never go near the jail," Mamma scolded. Leora had a feeling they shouldn't, but the excitement of getting those treasures seemed worth the risk.

The Goffs knew the deputy sheriff, so Mamma instructed the kids to go to the courthouse, confess their escapade, and ask whether they could still get the prizes from the inmates. The deputy escorted Merl and Leora to the jail. He ordered Merl to carry out some ashes first, perhaps to atone for their misdeeds. Then he unlocked the door and opened it wide enough for the men to reach out with the little cardboard schoolhouse, about 10" × 12", for Leora. Merl's treasure was a merry-go-round with cut-out animals. They'd also made a doll cradle and a church for the other two girls.

The kids thanked the men and headed for home, relieved and happy with their keepsakes. They never bothered a jail again.

CHAPTER 16

A Baby Sister and the Guthrie County Fair (1900)

A sweaty Pa, wearing dusty overalls and a layer of chaff, had threshed all day August 21. When he pulled in on a horse, his kids ran to meet him to announce a surprise. A new baby sister.

Leora was just the right age to enjoy rocking Ruby Belle and playing with her, but didn't get to often enough. Mothering was like that, with so many chores to do. Now Pa and Mamma had four sons and three daughters.

When the crew arrived to thresh at their place, usually for two or three days, the Goffs had to feed about twenty tired men for dinner and even supper. Neighboring farm women helped with all the cooking and baking during those sultry days. Flies were terrible pests. Someone with a dishtowel had to shoo them from the doorway, especially in the evening.

The three-day Guthrie County Fair provided a break for families every September. It's a good bet that Pa took at least his older youngsters with him. Mamma sent fried chicken in a basket for their dinner, also sandwiches, cake or cookies, and a jug of lemonade.

The merry-go-round always drew a crowd. Merl noticed that the ticket-taker tossed the used tickets on the ground, out of the way. He and another boy sneaked into the area and, when the merry-go-round was stopped, they crawled under it. They gathered the discarded tickets handing them out to the other kids. Until Leora's tattling put a stop to the dangerous trick.

The Guthrian, September 6, 1900

William Jennings Bryan ran against President William McKinley that November. McKinley won again.

CHAPTER 17

Two Moves, Two More Babies (1901-1902)

The jail episode may have been just one of many incidents, and maybe a lack of regular chores for the kids, that convinced the Goff family to move back to the farm south of Guthrie Center the spring of 1901. Leora was so glad to get back to bluebirds in the budding timber and her friend Verna Davis.

About once a week, a horse-drawn grocery wagon hauled wares to sell or trade from farm to farm. Mamma traded eggs and chickens for things she needed. The kids always liked to see the wagon come because they usually were treated to candy.

Sticks of paraffin, a penny each, were chewy like gum. Along rural roads, kids found ironweed, or gumweed as they called it, and broke the stems for the juice. In a day or two, the resin-flavored juice dried and was pleasant to chew.

Peddlers, usually Middle Eastern, often stopped by, some on foot carrying a heavy load, some with a one-horse rig. One pulled a cart with two horses. They brought everything from pots and pans to clothing. The kids were always excited to see him coming, with the harmonicas and all sorts of toys, but Mamma was ambivalent about their visits, especially when Pa was gone.

One time late in the fall, one arrived when Sherd was home. It snowed while the man was there, and since he was a regular, Pa invited him to stay overnight. The next morning, he carried out a religious ceremony in the house. He said the barn was too cold, and wanted the family just to go about their work. Sherd answered, "No, we will wait quietly while you perform your ceremony."

What an assortment of stuff the peddlers brought, a lot of it outdated. Pa bought Wayne, age 9, a suit for going to town. Wayne never liked that suit so as soon as he outgrew it, he just wore it for every day.

Hazelnut bushes and brush were abundant on those rolling hillsides south of Guthrie Center. Hazelnuts grew in clusters with rough prickly shells. Red-tailed hawks sailed high above the woodland. Every autumn, following the first frost, folks formed nutting parties and hiked into wooded areas to gather black walnuts.

That winter, Grandpap and Grandmother Goff (John B. and Florence) lived with Sherd and Laura and their seven children. It wasn't uncommon for three generations to live under one roof.

The next spring, restless Sherd sold the farm south of Guthrie Center, then rented the Dunley farm north of town, even though Laura was about to give birth again. Traditional moving day for farm families was March 1.

Willis Walter Goff was born March 8, 1902. It's a good thing that Pa's folks stayed with them then, so Grandmother Florence could help with everything. Leora was 11, Merl 10, Wayne 9, Georgia almost 8, Jennings 6, Rolla 3, Ruby 1 ½, and now another little one. This may have been the time the doctor told Sherd that having so many babies so close together was too hard on his wife. They also had a hired girl during this time.

That spring, Leora took on the job of caring for the setting hens, ones that brooded their eggs to hatch. Leora certainly enjoyed her job, as she'd always helped her mother with it before. She liked taking care of baby chickens and knew how to get a reluctant hen to "sit" on her eggs: Pluck up the hen and give her a ride, like a cartwheel in the air, until she is dizzy. She'll sit.

When she was 11, Leora experienced a "picture show" for the first time, at a schoolhouse five or six miles north of Guthrie Center. Merl, Wayne, Jennings, Georgia, as well as Mamma wanted to see this amazing new thing. They watched a train in motion, the first moving picture show for them all.

"The clatter of the corn harvester is heard in the land and the corn shocks begin dotting the fields." From *The Guthrian*, September 5, 1902.

The news noted that someone had "left a grip at the grove meeting at Monteith. They can have same by calling at the store."

"The basket meeting at Monteith came off as per arrangement and a mammoth affair it was." Folks looked forward to this gathering for weeks. "Although the roads were very dusty, the grounds were far enough away that no dust reached the vast congregation gathered in the shade of the trees.

"In the forenoon the service consisted of singing followed by an able sermon on 'The Foundation of the Christian Church'. After this the well filled baskets were opened and dinner was served. And such a dinner it was that none need to have gone home hungry, and if they did it was their own fault. To look at the long tables filled to overflowing it did not look like the 'down-trodden farmer' was there.

"Afternoon services consisted of the Lord's Supper, followed by a song service, after which the congregation listened to another able sermon on 'The Great Trumpet'. Both sermons were delivered by the pastor, Rev. Dunkleberger. At the close of the services the audience retired to the river near by where two converts were baptized. The audience then dispersed to their homes feeling that these annual meetings are a producer of much good feeling and brotherly love. "

A "basket meeting." Grandpap and Grandmother Jordan sometimes helped host these lengthy gatherings at the Monteith Christian Church, even housing ones from out of town.

The Jordans had an orchard with several varieties of apple trees. They stored apples in the cellar during winter. Every autumn, they dried apples and corn. The Goffs and the Jordans also canned everything they could in glass Mason jars.

Canning meant keeping the kitchen range hot for several hours, with a kettle filled with several jars at a time simmering in water, usually an hour or more, to make sure the precious food was safely preserved for winter. Leora helped with the entire process, from picking produce, collecting and washing the glass jars, to keeping an eye on her younger siblings.

President McKinley, who beat William Jennings Bryan in two presidential elections, was assassinated in September, 1901. He was succeeded by Vice President Theodore Roosevelt.

October skies surround Iowa with such vivid blue, a backdrop for a rich   vista of russets and brown, with leafy squirrels nests high in the oak and silver maple trees.

Another job on the Goff farm, after the small grain was threshed, was to fill muslin ticks, similar to huge pillow shams, with the remaining straw. Those were their mattresses until after next year's threshing. When the straw was ready, Mamma emptied the ticks of last year's, washed and dried them.

"Leora." Mamma unpegged the large ticks from the clothesline. "You older ones, please take these to the straw stack and fill them as full as you can."

"Sure, Mamma. Our beds will be so soft and smell so fresh tonight! Merl, Georgia! One more, Wayne? Let's go!"

They each filled one tick with fresh hay, then pushed and shoved and pummeled it so that more would fit. The youngsters helped each other, trying to make sure their mother would praise them for their endeavors. She did just that, but then leveled them off herself and was always able to stuff in more.

A hard job was finished, but how comfortable those new mattresses felt during long winter nights. Their pleasant outdoor aroma reminded them of warmer days.

CHAPTER 18

Key West, Minnesota (1903)

In the spring of 1903, Pa decided they'd move to northern Minnesota. As early as 1896, newspapers carried ads: "Red Lake Reservation Grand Rush for Homes–in Northern Minnesota, East and North of Grand Forks, ND. . . Special rates. . . lowest standard first class fare. . . home-seekers excursions. . ."

Neighbors had been up to check out the area. They came back with glowing reports of wonderfully fertile farm ground in one of the flattest valleys on Earth in Minnesota's Red River Valley. The area was already crisscrossed with drainage ditches running west to the slow-flowing Red River. That sounded especially promising to men trying to farm Guthrie County's rolling hills, which eroded with every "gully-washer."

Sherd Goff and others had been burned once, bankrupt after trying to get started in Nebraska, but Minnesota sounded lush and more hopeful. Five or six Guthrie County families relocated together: George and Libbie Wright (Libbie was a first cousin of Laura Goff), Bert Branson (cousin), Bertie and Estella Branson (also cousins), and Charles Mingus.

Pa sold off livestock and other items and bought a farm. Traveling by railroad, he and his father took livestock up first. The day after they left Iowa, Mamma–in a "family way" again– and Grandmother Goff started out with the eight children.

When they got to Grand Forks, North Dakota, to change trains, everyone but Mamma had come down with colds.

The Northern Pacific Railroad ran right through Key West, which was 13 miles east of Grand Forks. By the time Grandpap Goff met them there with a cutter loaded with comforters, a sudden blizzard had popped up. Even though their new home was only half a mile north, Leora said that arriving in a blizzard mixed up her sense of direction the whole time they lived in Minnesota.

They were still in the United States, but just 80 miles from the Canadian border.

That far north, there was no school during the winter, since the weather was too severe and dangerous. The school year began shortly after the Iowans arrived. The teacher and the children seemed foreign to the Goff children. *Minnesota: A State Guide*, by the WPA's Federal Writers' Project, said that there was a new tide of immigration in north and western portions of Minnesota in 1903, and that Norwegians, who rarely settled in areas of Swedish concentration, bought farms in the valley.

Polk County, Minnesota, was so flat that when Leora and her siblings were introduced at school, the teacher told the class that the new children had seen hills. Leora was puzzled that the local children acted jealous about it.

The huge Agassiz glacier is the reason that area is so flat. Even the 1910 plat map of Polk County shows canals or ditches every mile or so. Those canals and the area rivers run west into the Red River, then north all the way to Canada's Hudson Bay.

From Key West, the Northern Pacific spur track headed north, just east of the Goff home. In spring, when the snow melted it filled ditches next to the railroad track, which ran not far from the schoolhouse. Kids fastened rail ties together for a raft, then floated along during recess. The Goff kids also made a rail-tie raft at home.

At noon on nice days, if a flatcar were near the school, the students shoved it until it rolled well, then jumped on for a ride.

One day the bell rang for school when the kids were quite a way down the track. They abandoned the flatcar and ran back to school. A section man told the teacher to not permit them to play on the flatcars, afraid someone would get hurt.

Minnesota: A State Guide noted that railroads promoted large-scale wheat farming, with bonanza farms in the Red River valley averaging 2000 acres. Every railroad station had a terminal elevator, as did Key West.

The Goffs' house was a half mile north of Key West in a grove of trees. It was close enough to the church in town that folks came from miles around for gatherings in the Goffs' lush grove of trees. Horses and buggies parked everywhere. Area schools took part, with the children reciting for a program, contests, and lots and lots of food.

The house at Key West, taken several years later

Leora recited "The Clown's Baby," which was twelve verses long. She doubted she could learn all of it, but the teacher said she knew she was able. So Leora "got busy on it, went over and over on it one night and then I woke up next morning, I knew it all."

Homemade ice cream and other items were sold for the benefit of the church. A dance was held that evening in Key West, probably in their Woodman Hall, as those Scandinavians were fond of "vigorous dancing."

Grandpap and Grandmother Jordan rode the train from Monteith to visit in August, bringing a trunk full of nice apples from home since the Goffs lived too far north for apple trees to thrive. It was such a big treat because they bought apples by the barrel during the winter.

Sisters Georgia and Leora enjoyed driving the rural roads with Grandpap in a one-seat buggy pulled by a horse. David Jordan was a jovial man and taught them songs, like "Ke-mo, ki-mo."

> "There was a frog lived near a pool
> Sing song ketcha ketcha ki-me oh
> He surely was the biggest fool
> Sing song ketcha ketcha ki-me oh
> Ke-mo, ki-mo Del-O-Ware
> Hee-ma ho and in come a salasicker
> Some time Penny went a link tum nip cat sing song
> Ketcha ketcha ki-me oh."

Those Iowa grandparents stayed three or four weeks, so there were several rides with Grandpap. Georgia and Leora took turns driving. One time Georgia had the horse on a trot and Grandpap, with a twinkle in his eyes, said, "Georgia, don't make the horse go so fast--we will get home too quick."

CHAPTER 19

School in the Winter, and Christmas (1903)

The town of Fisher, ten miles south, offered school during the winter. Pa learned that a blacksmith from there and his wife wanted a girl Leora's age to board with them for school, and to help with their small children. George Wright's youngsters were cousins of the Goffs. They attended school in Fisher during the winter, so Leora already knew kids there.

Leora packed her clothes, items for school, as well as paper and envelopes so she could write home. The folks Leora stayed with entertained often and were gone in the evening a lot. The kind missus was German and a good cook. Leora played their pump organ, and she enjoyed the two children, but she still got so homesick. It helped to ride home with the Wright cousins for the weekend.

But when her sister Georgia wrote, "Don't be homesick. You will soon be home setting hens for Mamma," that did it. Leora burst out crying. The missus consoled her.

One sunny Saturday morning, Leora and an older girl, about 18 or 19 years old, took the train to Grand Forks in order to catch the train to Key West. By the time they got to Grand Forks, a blizzard had struck. In that flat country, a blizzard is dangerous. All the trains were snowbound.

The older girl contacted her cousin who worked in Grand Forks. He took them to a hotel, where they stayed while the blizzard raged all night. He found someone from Key West, who was also stranded but planned to head home Sunday afternoon. The girls rode home with him in a sled drawn by a team of horses, arriving after dark.

Monday morning was bright and clear and cold. Pa and Leora bundled up and drove back to Fisher in a "cutter" sleigh and team. It was only ten miles but seemed like a hundred. Leora's stockings were frozen to her heels and she suffered from chilblains for some time after that.

Caused by repeated exposure to cold temperatures, chilblains are a painful skin inflammation with itching, swelling, and blisters. A pretty good cure for chilblains, which Leora learned from the missus, was to boil potato peelings and soak your feet with them.

Sometime in February, the blacksmith's brother came to help in the shop and needed to stay there. There wasn't enough room for Leora so they located another place she could board and watch a couple of children. The woman there acted almost aristocratic, asking Leora to do much of her housework while she just sat idly or went visiting. Leora hardly had time to do her schoolwork.

The man's bachelor brother, a partner in a hardware store, also lived with them. Leora hadn't been there very long when one night, someone tried to force her door open. He didn't say anything, but she figured it was the bachelor brother. It scared her. She didn't say anything to the couple, but wrote home about it. Pa went right after her. When the haughty woman asked why he was taking Leora home, Pa offered, "Well, Leora is so homesick she can't learn at school." She was so glad to get home.

———

The Bertie Burris family, with their two little girls, had visited the Goffs a few weekends. The Burrises invited all eleven Goffs to spend Christmas with them. They lived seven miles away, so

Pa and the older children arranged plenty of straw and comforters in the bobsled that nice clear morning. Most of them rode in the bobsled, carrying with them food they'd cooked to share. The Goff brothers got a sled for Christmas, so Merl, almost 11, tied it on behind the bobsled and rode until someone noticed his nose was frozen white.

Over halfway to Burris's, a sudden blizzard descended on them. When they finally arrived, all coated with snow, they piled out of the bobsled with the bigger kids carrying the little ones, and Mamma with the baby. Bringing the chill into the Burris home, they learned that Helen, their youngest, about two years old, was very sick.

The Burris daughters, Helen on the left

Their hired man, Artie Walters, who had moved with them from Iowa, had been up all night, riding a horse several miles to find a doctor, who had sent medicine for pneumonia.

It was too late for the Goffs to turn back in the storm, so Bertie helped Pa shelter the horse in a shed. Turkey roasted in the house and, with what the Goffs brought, they all had a hearty Christmas dinner. With all those children cooped up in the house, everyone was subdued. The storm blew over by the middle of the afternoon, Helen Burris was getting better fast when the Christmas visitors bundled up and left for home.

They were so thankful when they arrived home from a Christmas none of them ever forgot.

CHAPTER 20

Georgia Falls Down the Stairs (1904)

Since turkeys were common in Minnesota, the Goffs also raised them. Several times they attended a raffle and a dance at the community building, which was an effective way to sell the turkeys. The event, which always drew a large crowd, included refreshments with gallons of coffee made in a wash boiler.

Summers brought hordes of mosquitoes. Pa made "smoke smudge" by burning damp straw. At first the cows he'd brought from Iowa had to be driven into the smoke until they learned that it gave them relief from the mosquitoes. Those he bought in Minnesota came running to get into the smoke, holding their heads to the ground to avoid breathing the smoke.

Pa and Grandpap ran a threshing machine one year, hiring a man with a "cook car," since Minnesotans didn't cook for threshers in their homes, like Iowans did. The cook hooked his car onto the threshing machine engine to move from place to place. The Goff youngsters liked to watch him. The threshing crew ate at the cook car, which had benches along both sides of it where the hot, hungry men could relax to eat. They slept in a bunkhouse or a barn, each man bringing his own blanket. It was rumored that some of the farmhands had lice, head and body lice. Threshing was a noisy, dusty, dirty endeavor, but the Goffs had never heard of humans having lice.

Pa sold that threshing outfit and the second year he hired his harvesting done by a much larger machine. There were rivalries among the two or three threshers in the territory. Farmers stacked their grain, wheat and oats and barley, ready for the machines. Sometimes, they'd find iron objects in their stacks meant to sabotage the machine. Those Scandinavian immigrants seemed different, spiteful and jealous of each other. Leora described it as if they'd never grown up.

The Goffs took their children in threes for their portraits. When Mamma took Georgia, Jennings, and Rolla to a photographer in Grand Forks. Leora went along to help with the little ones, and to put finger curls in Willis's hair.

Ruby, Perry, and Willis Goff, taken in North Forks, 1904

They did some shopping while in a bigger town. Mamma bought an *Oxford Self-Pronouncing American Edition of the Holy Bible*, and Leora got her first ready-made dress, pink. They chose a dress for Georgia, since the girls were to be in a church program there was no time to make new dresses.

One day, Georgia's chore was making the beds upstairs. The job finished, she took hold of the posts of two beds and swung between them. But she lost her balance, fell, and somehow bumped her head. She sat at the top of the stairs, but fainted and tumbled down the steps.

Leora and her mother were working in the kitchen and heard a thump at the stair door. Georgia must have tossed something down, they thought, but when they checked, the nine-year-old rolled out unconscious. Mamma carried her daughter to a settee while Leora got a cloth and cold water. Georgia eventually came to, but felt sickish for a while. She had a bad bump on her forehead, but they never consulted a doctor.

CHAPTER 21

Another Circus, Another Move (1904)

"Which would you rather see, the Independence Day celebration or the circus?" Pa asked his kids. Both were coming to Grand Forks, only three days apart. "We can't go to both."

"The circus!" It was unanimous. The Ringling Brothers Circus, on their 1904 route, included towns in Wisconsin, Minnesota, North Dakota, Winnipeg (Canada), South Dakota, western Iowa, eastern Nebraska, Kansas, and Missouri. That was only during the month of July.

Pa and the boys fed and watered the livestock early, while Mamma and the older girls prepared dinner to take. The men hitched up horses to the lumber wagon, Mamma packed the dinner basket, and the older siblings helped the little ones with their suspenders and shoes. They made it to Grand Forks in time for the circus parade. After the parade, the big family found some shade and enjoyed their dinner before the "Big Show" started.

In 1904, construction began on the Panama Canal. Theodore Roosevelt was elected to a full term as president, by the largest landslide in history. Pa and Mamma and even the older Goff kids were rather homesick for Iowa.

They moved into the town of Fisher for the winter, enrolling the kids in school. Leora was in sixth grade. Most of the seats were double in Leora's room, which held four grades. Some children in Georgia's room had head lice. She came home with them, from hanging her wraps in the cloakroom. Mamma, who was appalled, washed Georgia's hair and kept checking. What a worry for a mother not used to such things.

Because of a shirt once tied to a stick to warn steamboats of a bend in the river, Fisher was first called "Shirt-tail Bend." Steamboat traffic flourished on the Red and Red Lake Rivers between Winnipeg, Canada, and Fisher's Landing. Then named for a civil engineer for the railroad company, who was sent there to survey for the laying of tracks to meet the boat traffic, the name was later shortened to Fisher.

Leora was 14 years old that winter. The young people sledded and ice skated on the frozen Red River. Pa paid a fee for their share of keeping snow off the skating area. It was a long and snowy winter.

In late February, Pa asked his kids, "Are you ready to go back to Iowa?" They were. He quickly sold their team of horses, two cows, and household goods. The family boarded the train to Iowa, staying overnight in a Des Moines hotel. The next day, March 8, was Willis's third birthday.

The Rock Island RR took them west to the *Liza Jane* branch train at Menlo. And the *Liza Jane* took them home, to the Monteith depot where Grandpap Jordan met them. Grandparents and aunts and uncles welcomed the family with hugs and home cooking.

Not long after the Goffs were back, they learned that much of where they'd lived in Minnesota had flooded. Most of the families who moved up there with the Goffs also eventually returned to Iowa.

Yes, Laura Goff was expecting another baby.

CHAPTER 22

Clabe Wilson's Family (1903-1907)

While the Goff family lived in Minnesota, Clabe's mother Georgia Wilson gave birth to a daughter. Florence Fern, called Fonnie, was born in March 1903. Clabe was 15 and his sisters, Rectha and Alice were 14 and 12.

Georgia's parents, Samuel and Martha Williams, also lived in Jackson Township, so her mother could help during that time.

A year later, 1904, according to the local newspaper, Clabe's father Dan must have had a stroke. He was only 36 but was a "very sick man." Clabe took over much of taking care of livestock, but Dan rallied and began buying purebred Duroc Jersey hogs. There is very little information about the family during this time, mostly from newspaper items, and so much of it was negative. Georgia Wilson joined the Morrisburg Christian Church in 1905, and she had some kind of illness, which the local newspaper called an "attack." It lasted a few weeks. She was just 41.

The paper announced that Dan Wilson bought the purebred Duroc Jersey Lafollette as a herd boar. He and Clabe were building a hog business, so much of their time was taking care of brood sows and piglets, feeding and keeping the farrowing area clean.

Georgia Wilson's mother died in late 1906. Two weeks later, Verna Pauline Wilson was born. Although Georgia's sister Emma Stotts lived nearby with a family of her own, Georgia could have certainly used her mother's support during that time. She surely was devastated by the loss of her mother.

The Panora Vedette reported in July, 1907, that Mrs. Dan Wilson was not well. Her oldest, Clabe at age 17, helped take care of his little sisters, sometimes diapering baby Verna.

"Mrs. Dan Wilson has been quite ill in Jackson township and has required the services of a nurse but she is improving some now. Miss Boblett has been caring for her."

A week later, she was slightly improving, and about the same by the next report.

By September, the "Dan Wilsons were enjoying a visit from paper hangers last week." Perhaps it was hoped that a make-over might help her feel better. It was just in time for her husband and son to hold their "First Annual Sale Duroc Jerseys" at Pleasant Ridge Farm.

The farm was described as five miles west of Linden, ten miles northwest of Redfield, five miles south of Panora, and 5 miles east of Monteith. Railroad timetables were listed from Linden and Monteith, with "free entertainment and livery from Linden and Monteith." Purchased hogs could be loaded to take home on train cars at Linden and Monteith. Free entertainment?

The first one on the list in a sale booklet was Lafollette (#36563), the herd boar that Dan Wilson had purchased the year before. Those red purebred hogs with droopy ears were known by their pedigree. Also listed was the boar's own pedigree, from Belle's Chief (#22727) and Bishop's Choice (#32020). "Study the pedigree of the aristocratic fellow and make it a point to come and name a price on him."

A "litter sister to Lafollette" was offered for sale, along with at least four bred by "D. R. Wilson & Son, Redfield": Lady Lafollette, Lady Lafollette III, Panora Bell 4th, and Clary Wilson. One hog was named Carrie Nation, for the radical member of the temperance movement who opposed alcohol and who was known for attacking taverns with a hatchet!

The large sale, listing 91 purebred swine, was held on October 1. Two days later, the paper reported "A $2,000 Hog. At Dan Wilson's sale of Duroc Jersey hogs Monday one hog brought the snug sum of $2,000. The purchasers were Hood & Baker of Dunlap, Iowa. The hog is Lafette [sic] No. 36563 and is a famous one among the red hog men."

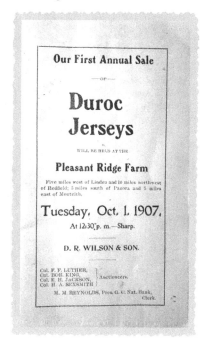

Cover of 1907 sale booklet

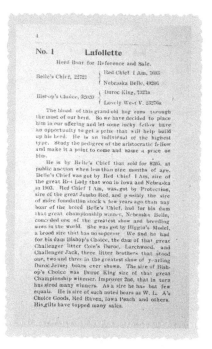

Page from the sale booklet

A $2,000 Hog.

At Dan Wilson's sale of Duroc Jersey hogs Monday one hog brought the snug sum of $2,000. The purchaser were Hood & Baker of Dunlap, Iowa. The hog is Lafette No. 36563 and is a famous one among the red hog men. This hog we are informed was sold to Mr. Wilson something like a year ago

Panora Vedette, October 3, 1907

CHAPTER 23

Home to Iowa (1905)

Those Guthrie County hills, covered with new spring-green leaves and white frothy blooms, were such a welcome sight. Meadowlarks were back already and cardinals had begun their boisterous spring calls. It was home.

Pa found a farm to rent northwest of Guthrie Center, along with machinery and livestock to purchase at farm sales. He hired out to do roadwork, leaving Merl and Wayne, ages 13 and 12, to do most of the farming. A neighbor, John Roberts, planted the corn, but those oldest brothers did the spring plowing and later cultivated the corn.

The rest of the family put in a big garden, even planting a cane patch in order to make sorghum molasses in autumn.

The Goffs' seventh son, Clarence Zenas, was born September 4, 1905, Ruby's very first day of school.

Grandmother Jordan came for a few days and Leora stayed home from school to help out. The morning after Clarence was born, no one could find Ruby. Leora eventually discovered her upstairs, hiding under the bed. She wanted to stay home with her baby brother, but Leora assured her that he'd still be there after school, that he was going to stay with them, and that Grandmother would still be there. That seemed to satisfy her, so she got ready to walk to school with eleven-year-old Georgia, hand in hand.

The Goffs received their first rural mail delivery while they lived at that farm. The mail carrier's team of small horses pulled a covered delivery wagon. It was a wonder not to wait until they went to town for groceries and to check for mail, which was usually once a week.

The Goff family lived there only a year, moving in March of 1906 to a farm in Audubon County, eight miles east and a little north of the county seat of Audubon, in Melville Township. Pa bought two cows from Grandpap Jordan,

and from a sale, he brought home fifteen heifers ready to calve that spring. Plenty of chores kept the family busy, since they also raised chickens and hogs. The kids named every milk cow— Rhoda, Genevieve, etc. They all helped plant and care for a large garden.

During harvest time, Georgia and Leora became cornhuskers and grainshockers with the men, while their father ran the grain binder.

The Goff kids hiked about a mile and a quarter north to Melville No. II country school, but the older boys attended only during the winter months.

Melville No. II country school, Audubon County, Iowa, 1906 L-R: Back: Ruth Estes, Marguerite Foley, Georgia Goff, Alice Estes, Eleanor Ohm (teacher), Leora Goff, Maude Ruhs, Lulu Leavens. Middle: Ruby Goff, Clara Foley, Pearl Ruhs, Lila Leavens, Zells Smith, Genevieve Crees. Hilda Ruhs. Front: James Crees, Edward Leavens, ? Estes, Harry Smith, Jennings Goff, Ambrose Foley, Rolla Goff. Absent: Merl and Wayne Goff, who were probably doing field work.

1907

All their crops were planted the spring of 1907. The Audubon newspaper told what happened in May: "We have had all kinds of weather the past week. Sunday [May 12] was very warm but exceedingly unpleasant because of the wind that blew the dust in all directions. One man put it the wind blew corn rows crooked. In fact, it was one of the worst we have ever seen of the kind. Monday was cooler and Tuesday was cold and Wednesday cooler still, with a little snow... The whole country is suffering more or less from the unusual cold and drought we are having this spring."

The wind blew all day and most of one night, the air filled with dust. A lot of seed was exposed and some blew away. It was a little late in the season to replant field corn, so Pa decided to plant popcorn since it has a shorter growing season.

That popcorn crop did so well that he continued raising it, along with field corn, oats, and hay. For several years, Pa contracted with a popcorn company each spring, in Chicago or Odebolt, to grow so many acres, the company furnishing the seed.

*Leora received a certificate for not missing class
for twenty consecutive school days in March 1907.*

At age 16, Leora Goff passed the eighth-grade exam. Audubon County held exercises that June for 54 graduates of rural schools. The thirty who were present to receive their diplomas were urged not to be satisfied until they'd obtained a high school education.

Leora had hoped to continue in high school but Pa declared that as the oldest of ten children, she was needed on the farm to help feed them all, help with the laundry, and help with the younger ones. And help in the fields. Sherd promised that his older kids were well-paid for their work instead of going to high school.

Leora Frances Goff, 8th Grade graduate, 1907,
J. F. Frazier's Studio, Audubon, Iowa

CHAPTER 24

Independence Day 1907

The only family portrait of all of the M.S. Goff family.
L-R: Back: Jennings (11), Georgia (13), Merl (15), Leora (16), Wayne (14),
Rolla (almost 9). Front: Ruby (almost 7), Milton Sheridan "Sherd" (about 42),
Perry (almost 4), Clarence (almost 2), Laura (about 39 and pregnant with
Virgil), Willis (5). July 4, 1907, Audubon, Iowa, J. F. Frazier's Studio

"We always had a big celebration of the 4th of July," Leora wrote in her memoir. "Nearly every town or burg had something doing. We used to get up at daybreak, get our work done—farm chores, and get ready to go to town by a team with a wagon or buggy. We would be in time to see the big parade and stay 'til the fireworks, generally, and then do farm chores when we got home. We were all tired but glad to have a big day.

"The 4th of July when I was 16 years old," that was 1907, "we eight older ones, Merl, Wayne, Georgia, Jennings, Rolla, Ruby, Willis, and I took the team and wagon with the feed for the horses, and our father and mother and the two youngest, Perry and Clarence, went in a one-horse buggy and had our basket dinner with them."

The residents of Audubon were awakened that morning by popping firecrackers and the boom of the old cannon–"saluting the forty-five states comprising our great republic," according to *The Audubon Republican* newspaper. That dew-drenched dawn, the Goffs fed their livestock and cleaned up. Ma probably fried chicken, most likely the first fryers of the year, and packed a dinner basket.

Accompanied by darting dragonflies and the chirp of crickets, the horses pulled the buggy and the wagon eight miles, over dirt roads and across the Nishnabotna River's wooden bridge, to town. Their horses joined dozens of others, tied up near the city park.

The newspaper said that the Audubon Martial Band met the train, which had steamed and chuffed to the station from the south, along Market Street. Off stepped members of the Atlantic Cornet Band at the depot, families with their dinner baskets, and the day's orator, Senator Shirley Gillilland of Glenwood, a handsome young man pictured with a large mustache.

It's easy to imagine the parade, led by the bands from Audubon and Atlantic, marching up Broadway Street to the city park at the top. What a perfect route for a parade, lined by men in suits, women in long-sleeved, high-necked dresses, the hems brushing the ground, children of all ages. The crowd followed and gathered around the stand in the park, the paper said, with "no buildings around to interfere."

At 9:45, the Atlantic Band gave a concert of "a high class of music." Next a chorus sang patriotic songs, a reverend offered a prayer, and a school boy recited Lincoln's Gettysburg address.

Then, according to the newspaper, in a strong voice and with a commanding personality, Senator Gillilland made a forty-minute address that held the attention of the crowd "circumspect in character and conduct." The only criticism was that the speech was too short.

Picnicking began at noon. Afterwards the men checked on the horses, and the youngsters and older folks probably napped on old quilts.

"While we were eating our dinner," wrote Leora, "the folks thought of having a family picture taken while we were all together. Pa was the only one of the men or boys who had a tie on, and Rolla wanted to go barefoot as he claimed his shoes hurt his feet. I expect they did as he went barefoot most always. So we went to the picture studio for the picture and Rolla's bare feet showed in the picture. It was the only family picture we ever had taken of us all."

Sports contests began at 1:30—races (even one for fat men of at least 210 pounds), shot put, tug of war, sack race, pole vault, wheelbarrow race, a drill team, and a baseball game between Audubon and Dedham on the grounds near the electric light plant. (Audubon won 7-1.) There were cash prizes but no Goffs were named among the winners.

"The day ended with a rain shower in the late p.m. There were no paved roads so we came home in the mud. Ruby wore white shoes [they don't look white in the photo] and she got them muddy, but all seemed happy anyway."

CHAPTER 25

Riding a Horse to Piano Lessons (1908)

In early 1908, the eleventh Goff baby was born, Virgil Cleon.

That August Miss Nora Brown, who had been in charge of music in the Audubon public schools, married Mr. Donald Preston. As was required in those days, she resigned her position with the public schools. But Nora Brown Preston began giving private music lessons.

Among her piano students on Saturdays was Leora Goff who, wearing a dress, rode a horse to her lessons, nine miles along those dusty roads. Purple thistles, often visited by black swallowtail butterflies, nodded along the way. Leora tied up the horse at a hitching post in front of the Preston home.

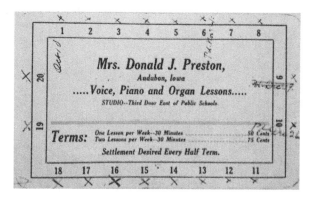

Record of payments for Leora's piano lessons, 1908

87

Even though the Goffs' rural church rarely had a minister come to speak, the family walked to Sunday School held at Melville Center. Leora began to play the pump organ for the hymns when the regular organist wasn't there.

Never robust, the Goffs' baby, Virgil Cleon, died just short of his first birthday. He was buried in Audubon's Maple Grove Cemetery.

Pa's folks, John B. and Florence Goff, followed their son Ed when he homesteaded in Oklahoma, then to South Dakota and on to Montana, where Grandpap had a stroke. Pa took the train to Bozeman, but his father had died April 5, 1909, before Pa arrived. Pa brought his body back for a funeral at the Monteith church, with his burial in the nearby pioneer cemetery.

CHAPTER 26

The 1909 Iowa State Fair

Probably because 1909 was the 55th anniversary of the State Fair, the legislature voted $100,000 for a new grandstand—for some 900 tons of steel plus plenty of cement and stone to build it. It's still in use today. Not only did the Iowa State Fair get a new grandstand, there was a new Administration Building that year, a new race track, and new sidewalks.

Wireless telegraphing flashed messages across the fairgrounds and motorcycle races were held for the first time. Iowa women rallied there for the right to vote.

"One summer," Leora remembered, "Pa and us four oldest—Merl, Wayne, Georgia, and I—went to the State Fair in August. We drove a team and buggy (carriage) to Grandpap Jordan's in Monteith and put the team in the barn and went on the Liza Jane train from Monteith to Des Moines."

Depot and train at Monteith, Iowa

Yes, the *Liza Jane* went all the way to Des Moines! That year the railroads offered special service with reduced fares "from every point in the state." Pa took advantage of this new deal.

You can imagine Pa ordering sons Merl (16) and Wayne (15) to hitch up the team early in the morning. And daughters Leora (17) and Georgia (14) packing a basket dinner, hitching up their skirts to climb into the buggy, and the five of them waving to Mamma and the younger ones left behind: Jennings (12), Ruby (8), Willis (6), Perry (5), and Clarence (3). Jennings was probably left behind to tend to the livestock.

The two dozen miles of country roads, lined with the glow of goldenrod and elderberries laden with dark fruit, led them through eastern Audubon County, across the Missouri-Mississippi River Divide west of Guthrie Center, and on to Grandpap's. They boarded the *Liza Jane* which took them to Menlo, then east on the mainline Rock Island track, all the way to the fairgrounds on the east side of Des Moines.

"It was a real jaunt for us four, and it sure was enjoyed. I remember there was a place where buttermilk was sold by the glass. Pa and I were the only ones who liked buttermilk and, of course, we looked at machinery and the stock barns, etc. We had to stick together and not get lost. We watched John Philip Sousa's Band—it was so wonderful, I remember. They played 'Stars and Stripes Forever.'"

I couldn't confirm that John Philip Sousa was indeed at the 1909 fair, but that year sprinkling carts kept the dust down, hundreds of benches were added and ten thousand tin cups were distributed to visitors. Admission was 50 cents.

"It was a big day and then we had to get a "Special" (train) to take Fair-goers back home from the fairgrounds to the Liza Jane train. We stayed overnight at Grandpap Jordan's and back to the Audubon County farm the next day, all happy."

CHAPTER 27

Clabe Wilson (1908-1909)

Clabe's sister Alice left the deteriorating situation in the Wilson home, married Ed McLuen in February 1908, and made a new home in Stuart.

Clabe Wilson was reported quite ill with appendicitis in March 1908, according to the local paper.

A month later, his Grandfather Samuel Williams died, leaving his pioneer farm to his daughters—Emma Stotts, Alice Wolfe, and Georgia Wilson—all having "comfortable homes on different portions of what formerly constituted the old homestead." The fourth daughter, Serepta Henderson, lived in Inman, Kansas.

Samuel Williams was buried with his wife Martha and other relatives in nearby Morrisburg Cemetery.

Two months later, Clabe's mother, Georgia Wilson, was reported "very sick" by the *Vedette*.

Even though Dan Wilson was listed in the *Iowa State Register and Farmer* as the exhibitor of three Duroc Jerseys at the 1908 Iowa State Fair, Dan Wilson's health was declining: July—attack of apoplexy (stroke), October—stroke.

Mid-January 1909, the *Vedette* told that "D.R. Wilson has been quite ill for some time. One day last week he had a stroke of paralysis and now is dangerously ill."

After the strokes, Dan Wilson could barely use his left arm. He sent a photo postcard of himself, with such a poignant note to his wife, "I am anxious to hear from you all love to you all from your best friend." It is written in Stuart, maybe from his daughter Alice's.

Daniel Wilson, from the February 1909 postcard

Perhaps Alice took him in after he threw a corn knife at Clabe, according to records from Clarinda State Hospital, where he was admitted a month later.

From the hospital records: "Likes and dislikes were too pronounced. A dislike for any person turned into intense hatred without sufficient cause. Is subject to attacks of frenzy when crossed. . .. Has threatened, but not attempted suicide."

Dan Wilson, age 42, had been a "periodical drinker to excess," and "domestic relations have never been pleasant." "Has always had a violent temper and inclined to fight." This certainly gives insight into what kind of father Clabe Wilson grew up with, what his mother and sisters had endured.

Dan was "considerably depressed" in March, though "neat and orderly and quite agreeable." He "got along very well for a week," then failed dramatically, dying the evening of April 3, 1909.

After Daniel Ross Wilson died at the state mental hospital, his remains were sent to Coon Rapids, where his mother still lived. He was buried at the east end of the Coon Rapids cemetery, under the bur oaks, among his pioneer ancestors and his twin brother, who had died at birth.

He left a widow at home (Georgia, age 44), adult children (Clabe and Rectha), and two small daughters (ages six and two). Plus a barnyard full of red hogs.

Ten days after Dan Wilson's death, his mother Emily Wilson died at Coon Rapids. She was Clabe's last grandparent.

Clabe's sister, Rectha, married Laura Goff's youngest brother, Frederick Jordan, in November. They made their home at Monteith.

CHAPTER 28

Mrs. Connrardy's Sewing School (1910)

The early 1900s was considered the golden era of postcards. Until telephones were more common, postcards were a cheap and cheerful way for families, neighbors, and friends to stay in touch. Mamma was known as a woman who could get more written on a postcard than anyone else.

Her daughters, Leora and Georgia, were fans of postcards to communicate with friends. In this way, they invited each other to evening parties, for music and dancing at home, or to act out their own plays. Often on Friday nights, especially during the winter, young people attended box socials and literary meetings. For box socials, the girls made supper and arranged it in a decorated box. Boys bid on the boxes, then enjoyed eating it with the girl who prepared it.

After several get-togethers, Leora received mysterious postcards with just someone's initials, or a comment about the party and a signature. Postcards were mailed to her in Minnesota, from someone she'd met when they lived there. Yes, she saved them all.

She received chatty postcards from girlfriends, some inviting her to a birthday party. The Goff children regularly received picture postcards from their grandparents for their birthdays and holidays.

Since Leora wasn't yet married, she was encouraged to take a six-week sewing class in Exira with her friend Katherine "Katie" Dutler in the spring of 1910. Katie's older sister had attended the school, then afterwards, families hired her to sew for them.

The girls boarded with Katie's elderly German aunt and uncle Jake Engle, who had no children, in exchange for help with laundry, ironing, and other chores.

Alice Connrardy ran a successful sewing school from about 1897 until 1925. She took sewing courses in Chicago at the Baughman School for Dressmaking, then trained girls and women at her home.

The Baughman Adjustable Tailor System included learning to draft patterns, in addition to using a sewing machine, handwork, and all about fabrics. Mrs. Connrardy, the wife of John B. Connrardy, a German immigrant and Civil War veteran who was elected Audubon County Sheriff twice, returned to Chicago occasionally for a refresher course.

Quite a bit of mail was addressed to Leora at Exira–at least twenty postcards from family and friends, and even a couple of boyfriends–Guy somebody and Carles or Carlos Ross.

The tail of Halley's Comet was easy to spot during the warm, clear evening while the girls lived in Exira. Georgia Goff sent her sister a newsy postcard from home, telling about seeing the long tail of the comet on three different nights.

"Mrs Connrardy, her assistant and sixteen pupils in dress-making went to Audubon Friday and had class pictures taken which they will highly prize as the years go by," according to *The Audubon County Journal*, May 26, 1910.

Leora did highly prize the group photo, carefully packing it as she relocated from home to home for decades.

The girls and their instructors rode the train to Audubon for a class picture. Photographed by Harper, most of the seamstresses were pensively leaning on their hands.

1910 Dress Makers: Katie Dutler is in the top left. Second row at right is
Mrs. Connrardy. Middle: Connrardy College, Leora Goff at right.
Bottom row: last two are Edith Christensen and Clara Lund.
Taken May 20, 1910, Harper, Audubon, Iowa

Another clipping from *The Audubon County Journal*, June 2, 1910:
"Mrs. Connrardy closed another term of her dressmaking school
last Saturday, the sixteen pupils receiving their diplomas that day
and departed for their respective homes."

When Leora wasn't needed at home for feeding threshers or
popcorn harvesters, she sewed for people in the area, sometimes
staying with the family while she worked.

A postcard noted that Sherd Goff went to Chicago one evening to get popcorn seed, planning to plant 75 acres of it. He made enough money raising popcorn to purchase a farm in Guthrie County, northeast of Wichita and northwest of Guthrie Center. They still had one more year on the lease in Audubon County, so they stayed put until the next spring.

CHAPTER 29

Wichita, Iowa (1911)

The house in Audubon County was devoid of trees when the Goff family moved there in 1906. The family dug up volunteer saplings along the country roadsides and planted them in the yard. By the time they left five years later, those little trees were thriving. This was the longest they'd live in any one place.

The house where the Goffs moved to near Wichita, northwest of Guthrie Center, the spring of 1911, was much larger, with a shady yard which bloomed with roses and lilacs. A Catalpa tree, a walnut grove, an orchard, and evergreens enhanced the house and outbuildings.

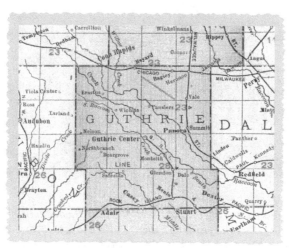

A 1911 map showing Audubon, Wichita, Guthrie Center, Monteith, Panora, Glendon, and Stuart. Clabe's chapters also mention Coon Rapids (which Clabe reached on ice skates via the Raccoon River), Redfield, and Linden.

The farm was near the Wichita church, where the family attended, a grocery store and a school. Rolla, Ruby, Willis, Perry, and Clarence attended the Wichita school until they graduated from eighth grade.

The neighbors' young folks often gathered at the Goff home for music, singing, and party plays. On nice Sunday afternoons, they played baseball in the big yard.

During the week, the family stayed busy with gardening, farming, chores, cooking, cleaning the house, mending, filling and cleaning oil lamps, washing, hanging out dresses and overalls and bedding, and ironing. As their plentiful fruits and vegetables ripened, Mamma and her girls began the hot job of canning for winter.

"A bunch of folks at the Goff residence at Wichita" (Georgia Goff's writing)
No date. Ruby is second from left, then Willis, Georgia, Perry, Merl, their
mother Laura, Clarence, Sherd, next two unidentified. Jennings is at right.

Georgia and Leora Goff, July 15, 1911,
probably taken at Guthrie Center

Ruby and Georgia Goff, July 15, 1911

Georgia and Leora Goff, July 15, 1911, the hats
were probably photographer's props

CHAPTER 30

Popcorn King of Guthrie County

Known as the "popcorn king" of Guthrie County, Pa's name was often mentioned in the local newspaper along with his crops and travels. "M.S. Goff hauled the last of his popcorn and carred it for the Kansas City market this week." (*The Guthrie Times*, Jan. 24, 1912)

Perhaps someone from the local paper contacted him for news. February 1, 1912: "M.S. Goff bought a team of horses this week."

Leora began staying more often with her elderly grandparents at Monteith. She later stayed three weeks in Guthrie Center with her mother's youngest sister, Cora Parrish and her new baby boy, named Boyd.

That year, Merl and Wayne farmed land east of the Goff home and they needed a housekeeper during the day. Leora bicycled 2 ½ miles every day, gathering dead wood from the grove to use in the cooking range, along with corn cobs. She cooked and cleaned for them in part of the R. G. Gingery house. The Gingery family lived in the rest of the house.

The sinking of the RMS *Titanic* in the Atlantic was in the news that spring. Leora was anxious to bike home to read the latest about it.

She became her brothers' barbers because they didn't want their father clipping their hair too short. With seven brothers, it was a good thing they didn't all want haircuts the same day.

"M.S. Goff is building a double corncrib." (Oct. 10, 1912)

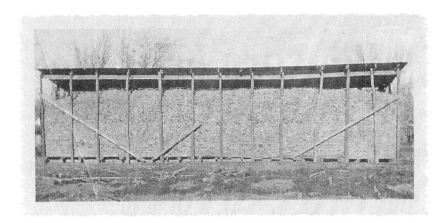

Sherd Goff's crib, full of popcorn, 48 feet long

New Mexico and Arizona became states in 1912. Now there were 48 white stars in the American flag which school children would pledge allegiance to for decades.

Leora stayed with her Jordan grandparents during the week-long Baptist Association meetings held at the Monteith church. Grandpap enjoyed those so much, but the women were kept very busy. People came from all over and stayed in homes in the area, including the Jordan home. That meant feeding them three meals a day. There was no refrigeration, Leora wrote in her memoir, "so we had to get beef or meat from the meat wagon which came 2 or 3 times a week, and kill some chickens." When the meat wagon didn't come on time, she'd kill and clean the chickens herself.

The women also baked bread, made noodles or dumplings, and gathered and cleaned vegetables from the garden, with help from those who were able. There was no indoor plumbing, so they carried water for cooking and cleaning, and their outhouse was kept busy. Leora noted that "it was a joy for those who didn't do the cooking or washing."

CHAPTER 31

Grandpap Jordan Dies (1913)

Grandpap David Jordan died February 11, 1913, age 71. In 1887, according to his obituary, he'd been baptized "into the fellowship of the church of Jesus Called Sharon of Regular Predestinarian Baptists."

David Jordan

"Brother Jordan was liberated to preach wherever God in his providence cast his lot which he continued to do as long as his health permitted when ever opportunity opened the door preaching Christ and him crucified as the only way to the father, the perfect, complete and only Savior of sinners and that there is salvation in no other for there is no other name given under heaven or among men whereby we must be saved.

"Without courting the favor of men with entire indifference to both censure and applause of men, he preached the doctrine of Christ in its simplicity and not in the letter but in the spirit. His generous hospitality endeared him to all his brethern [sic] and friends for brother Jordan's house was open to them at all times.

"His life was an open book to all who knew him and he was a living epistle known and read of all men, and we feel sure that he is not lost but gone and our loss is his eternal gain. He was known and loved by all the churches in Iowa and eastern Nebraska having visited probably all of them and preached Christ to them.

"He leaves to mourn his loss, two brothers, Francis of Monteith [married Emily Stringer], Sidney G. [married Sarah Hughes, then Emily Jane Bell] of this county, five sisters, Eliza Reed [Mrs. Harmon Talley Reed] and Mrs. G. B. [Clarissa] Hook of Long Beach, California, Mrs. Lem [Nancy] Fowler of South Dakota, Mrs. C. A. [Sarah] McCoy of Washington, and Mrs. Caroline Rainey of Ohio. His wife, four daughters, Mrs. [Lottie] Anderson of Palisade, Mrs. [Laura] Goff, Mrs. F. F. [Floy] Cowden and Mrs. J.E. [Cora] Parrish of Guthrie county, three sons, Frederic D. and Floyd R. of Monteith, and Collis of Palisade, Colorado . . ." {From *The Guthrie Times*]

A mile-long row of horses and buggies lined the dirt road around Monteith for his funeral and burial in the cemetery near where he'd farmed most of his life.

CHAPTER 32

Leora Meets Clabe

Leora stayed with her widowed grandmother in Monteith.. Grandmother's youngest son, Fred Jordan, just a year older than Leora, had married Rectha Wilson. They lived in Monteith and, just before Grandpap Jordan died, welcomed their first baby, named Leonard Clabe Jordan.

Clabe Wilson was at his sister's one day when Leora and Grandmother came to call. That is how Clabe and Leora met.

In June, 1913, he sent her a tentative "Good Luck" postcard, signed "C.D.W." That's all that was on it. I guess it was his way of letting her know he was interested.

It evidently worked. She replied with a "To Greet You" card. "Dear friend," it began, then some chitchat, ending "Answer soon. L.G. Guthrie Center."

Their first real date was to the Chautauqua in Panora, traveling there (and everywhere else) by horse and buggy. Chautauquas were a popular form of adult education and entertainment across the nation during the late 19th and early 20th Centuries.

The Chautauqua at Panora advertisement offered "a new set of delightful surprises every day" to the citizens of Guthrie County. "Fine education and uplift. It's an educational picnic." An easy way for shy Clabe to get acquainted with Leora.

1913 Newspaper announcement for the Chautauqua in Panora

Both of Clabe Wilson's sisters nearest his age were married by 1909, so he lived with his widowed mother and two much younger sisters, whom he'd cared for when his mother was too ill.

Still a bachelor at age 26, he probably felt awkward meeting Leora, as he did with new people. Leora grew up in a large gregarious family who enjoyed visiting and having rousing discussions. She could start a conversation with anyone, a winsome asset when talking with a handsome man of few words.

For one date, they planned to spend the day at Dexfield Park, which was between Redfield and Dexter. It commenced to sprinkle while they were there. The roads would become muddy quickly, so they left in a hurry.

The Monteith Methodist Church

In December, they attended the Christmas sermon and program at the Monteith Christian church. Afterwards, Clabe gave Leora a silver vanity set—mirror, brush, and comb.

"Oh dear. Clabe, I didn't get you anything."

"I know something I'd like to have, the Home Sweet Home you painted."

She gladly gave him the painting on velvet, with red roses entwined with the words.

And he asked her to be his bride. She said yes.

CHAPTER 33

Leora Gets Married (1914)

Clabe Wilson and Leora Goff were married in the Goff home near Wichita on February 15, 1914. The noon wedding was late because the minister, John Carl Orth from Guthrie Center, had a difficult time getting through the eight miles of snow drifts with his team and buggy.

Wedding photo, probably taken in Guthrie Center. Clabe and Leora Wilson

No one from Clabe's family near Panora, Monteith, or Stuart could get there to share the happy day. Georgia Goff was the bridesmaid, and Merl Goff was the best man.

From *The Guthrie Times*, February 19, 1914:

A QUIET HOME WEDDING

Last Sunday, February 15, 1914, a quiet home wedding was celebrated at the home of Mr. and Mrs. M.S. Goff, near Wichita, Seeley township. It was the giving in marriage of the daughter of the home, Miss Leora Frances Goff to Claborn [sic] Daniel Wilson. On account of illness in the family there were only the immediate friends of the contracting parties present. The ceremony that joined the happy young people together was read by John C. Orth, pastor of the First Presbyterian church of Guthrie Center. At the close of the beautiful service the company was invited to the dining room where an elegant wedding dinner was served, all enjoying the feast . . . "

In addition to the drifting snow, there was indeed "illness in the family." Merl thought he might have caught mumps at a picture show in Guthrie Center. He had recovered, but Perry and Clarence came down with them. Leora felt a swelling on her neck and jaw that morning, although her folks thought she'd already had mumps as a baby.

A couple of weeks after the wedding, Clabe experienced a light case of mumps. A shivaree, a noisy mock serenade for newlyweds, planned by the neighbors was called off when they learned they might catch the disease.

Clabe and Leora began their life together with a few furnishings. Leora had made some quilts and collected other household items. Clabe had a set of Rogers silverplate, with oak leaves on the handles, a 100-piece set of dinnerware, and even some furniture. And there was Leora's "Home Sweet Home" picture.

The young couple made their first home on the old Jordan farm, half a mile west of Monteith. Leora knew the house well. She was the third generation in her family to live there.

The Jordan house, which replaced a log cabin in 1882, ½ mile west of Monteith, 1976. (The same house is in the background in the 1897 photo of the Jordan family.)

Clabe hung their wedding portraits and the "Home Sweet Home," among other keepsakes that followed the couple from home to home throughout the ups and downs of the decades.

Clabe raised Chester White hogs, his favorites, twenty of them. And purebred Duroc Jerseys, which his father had been famous for.

Leora's folks spent two days in Des Moines in March, attending an auto show and a thresherman's association meeting. Pa made a deal for a second-hand Buick, stopping on their way home to Wichita to show it off for Clabe and Leora.

Georgia Goff wrote to her sister that Pa and another man were gone overnight on business. As soon as their father was out of sight, Jennings (age 18) took his older brother Wayne for a spin in the Buick, "all around the yard and through the old corn crib several times, then Merl and Jennings drove it down the road west and came back. Then Merl took a turn at the wheel and took the three little kids on a merry ride around the yard a few times."

The sisters took a turn riding. Georgia thought the cylinders would fly out and roll away. Jennings "has the record of being a speeder," she noted. "Come up and have a ride before the auto dies."

By the end of July, wheeler-dealer Sherd Goff had brought home a new ice box, and he'd traded his Buick for a new Cadillac.

As talk of a war in Europe heated up after the Archduke of Austria had been assassinated earlier in the summer, the United States declared neutrality. And the Panama Canal opened.

Mr. and Mrs. Clabe Wilson, in front of the Panora home of his mother and two youngest sisters

CHAPTER 34

Grandmother Jordan Dies, Willis's Accident (1914)

DEATH OF MRS. EMELIA JORDAN

"Emelia Ann Moore was born Dec. 27, 1846, and died August 17, 1914, at the home of her daughter, Mrs. Herb Cowden, near Casey, Iowa. She was united to David Jordan January 5, 1868. Seven children are left to mourn the loss of a dear mother: Mrs. Laura Goff, Wichita, Iowa, Mrs. Floy Cowden, Casey, Iowa, Mrs. Lottie Anderson of Palisade, Colo., Mrs. Cora Parrish of Guthrie Center, Floyd Jordan of Gendon, Frederic Jordan of Panora, Iowa, and Collis Jordan of Palisade, Colo. She united with the Baptist church in 1887, of which she was a faithful member to the last. . ." [From *The Guthrie Times*, August 27, 1914]

Emelia Jordan was the grandmother Leora had lived with at Monteith.

By September, the local paper reported that "M. S. Goff has the old east addition of his house removed [kitchen and dining room] and is going to build 'higher and wider'."

Fourteen-year-old Ruby wrote to Leora that everyone at home was well except for their younger brother, twelve-year-old Willis.

The family had visited the Ed Taggarts, where Willis and the Taggart boy decided to catch ponies to ride. When Willis rode one bareback, it started for a fence and turned short, throwing him into a barbed wire fence. It ripped his shirt nearly off, tore his suit, and cut a gash on top of his head about an inch deep, clear to the skull. He also had a slit on his back about a foot long "that you could lay your finger in," and his back and arms were cut and scratched.

Merl raced them to the doctor in Audubon, at 52 miles per hour. Willis was scared when Dr. Brooks put three stitches in his head, but he didn't whimper.

Uncle Ed Goff, Sherd's brother, brought Grandmother Goff back to Iowa from Montana. She visited friends while he helped husk corn. They both visited the Ben Black family, who were relatives who had a new baby since they'd last seen them.

For Leora's 24th birthday, she received postcards from her mother, sister Georgia, eleven-year-old brother Perry, and nine-year-old brother Clarence.

Mamma invited "C.D.W. & L.F.W." to Christmas dinner at the parental home via picture postcard.

Another postcard from Georgia urged her sister to come up for New Years in "that cute little sled."

CHAPTER 35

Delbert Wilson Born (1915)

The Jordan homestead was sold for the first time since David and Emelia Jordan had built a log cabin there in 1868, so Clabe and Leora moved to the farm her father owned, which had been the pioneer home of her great grandfather Ephraim Moore. The land had changed owners several times, but it was the same place the Goffs lived when Leora was about seven years old.

In order to keep track of when baby chicks would hatch, Leora began keeping an account of the dates her hens began to brood, laying no more eggs but sitting on their nests to hatch the eggs which took about three weeks. She recorded the number of other eggs she gathered, in order to sell or trade what they didn't use. Besides having a source of income, she enjoyed working with a flock of chickens.

In May, a German U-boat sank the British liner *Lusitania*, with 128 Americans aboard. When President Wilson protested, his Secretary of State William Jennings Bryan thought he was too aggressive, so he resigned. The Populists opposed war, and the Midwest was isolationist.

Delbert Goff Wilson was born at this place June 3. The doctor was there and so was Leora's mother, who helped administer ether when contractions were severe. Delbert was the first grandchild for Sherd and Laura Goff.

Throughout her life, Leora longed for a home of her own and to live near family. She was blessed by her folks and siblings close enough to visit often.

The well water near their house was rusty, so they hauled water from a spring on the edge of Beaver Creek, using a big wooden barrel on skids dragged by horses. The house had no running water for cooking, cleaning, and the weekly clothes washing, so this was an added chore.

Clabe's mother lived in Panora, with no way to get around. Two of her sisters lived in the area, but they had families of their own. Georgia Wilson hired "auto livery" to take her to Guthrie Center, to Morrisburg on Sunday (church), and once to southwest of Monteith, which may have been to see her daughter Rectha and her two small children.

Besides news of cooking for a big threshing crew, Georgia Goff wrote to her sister that Fred Schlotterbecks had a new piano, that the Dowd store sold pianos in Guthrie Center for "$50 and up." A Mr. Eddy planned to bring them a cornet for Jennings after Chautauqua, and that their mother Laura, who had a lovely alto voice, had attended a singing school, which was under the leadership of Mr. Eddy.

The Guthrie Times reported that "Quite a number of our young people are taking music lessons of Mrs. Eddy of Guthrie Center. They are a wide awake bunch and know a good thing when they see it."

A November paper noted that Sherd Goff and part of his family were moving "from their fine farm near Wichita to Guthrie Center." Their sons would stay to open the farm come spring, but "Sherd and the Mrs. have worked long and successfully and deserve a long and pleasant vacation." Sherd was only 50 years old. (They didn't move until 1918.)

The Wilsons had a telephone by the end of 1915. Georgia tried to ring them through the Monteith switchboard. She could hear the operator ring them: one long and three shorts. No answer. It was a party line, with neighbors on the same line. Each phone had a different ring, but they soon learned which ring was for which neighbor and sometimes listened in.

Georgia had tried to call in hopes that Clabe and Leora and baby Delbert could come for Christmas. Wichita was about fifteen miles by horse and buggy, but the three of them were able to attend.

Delbert was the only baby at the Christmas program, with his aunts vying to hold him. He fell asleep until Edith Lathrop sang a loud note in "Eventide," which woke and scared him. When he wouldn't quiet down, the minister suggested they take him to the parsonage, so that's where the little family spent the rest of Christmas Eve services.

The Guthrie Times, December 30, 1915: Wichita M. E. Church. "Another great event! The Christmas Tree at this place a success in every way, the tree itself was a large evergreen while the decorations were most beautiful. There were many pretty as well as useful presents.

"The program which was composed of songs by the choir, recitations by the boys and girls, ending in a beautiful drill, was pronounced by all present as being (at least) one of the best ever put on at Wichita.

"After the program Santa Claus came in with candy and nuts for all the children and some older ones.

"The people of Wichita do not believe in doing things by halves… "

And a memorable evening for Leora, as she wrote about it decades later.

Tragedy for Cousins (1916)

Pa owned another farm "down on Beaver," 129 acres. The Goffs lived there when Rolla was born in 1898. It had been remodeled, with a handy windmill near the house now. Clabe and Leora moved there in the spring of 1916.

Leora sure stayed busy with nursing a baby, cooking, cleaning, washing and ironing, and tending her chickens. She sold eggs seven dozen at a time early in the year, then twenty-four dozen each time by March. By July, this businesswoman had sold 350 dozen eggs, then she began selling chickens.

The mercury in thermometers during July and early August reached 100 degrees. During that suffocating heat, with no electric fans, cousins of the Goffs, Ben and Mattie Black, faced a tragedy. All six of their children became terribly sick, with what some thought was caused by eating green apples.

William Black, almost five years old, died. Three days later, a sultry day reaching 102 degrees, Robert (3) and Martha (not quite 2) also succumbed. Mamma and Pa took food to console them and attended the difficult funeral as well. Mamma wrote the devastating news to her daughter on a postcard, hoping that if Lucile (age 8) lived overnight, she'd get well.

The Guthrie Times, Aug. 10, 1915 - Southwest Guthrie: "At this writing a terrible tragedy is occurring at the home of Mr. and Mrs.

Ben Black just over the west Guthrie County lines in Melville township. They had a short week ago six bright, healthy children. Last week they buried their little boy, a child of five, perhaps. Sunday, last, the sixth inst., two others were laid away, while at present the three remaining children are at the point of death.

"The doctors are nonplussed as to the nature of the disease, so we hear. A specialist from Council Bluffs, also one from Chicago has been called in consultation with the local physicians. The supposition seems to be that the disease is cholera or hydrophobia. Mr. Black's hogs were dying with cholera. The family dog ate the dead hogs, and it is thought the children were infected by playing with the dog."

The children were buried in Arlington Heights Cemetery in Audubon. The three other children eventually got well.

So many families had lost youngsters to disease, including both of Sherd's and Laura's folks. During those days, sickness always hovered as a background threat.

CHAPTER 37

Donald Wilson Born (1916)

That autumn, Pa advertised six Guthrie County farms for sale, from 40 to 360 acres (a total of 844 acres), from 4 ½ miles northeast of Stuart to eight miles southwest of Guthrie Center. It's doubtful that he was successful in selling them all.

Georgia addressed a letter from "Wichita Heights" on Ruby's 16th birthday. What a busy family. Merl and Pa were threshing near Stuart, and Willis was helping stack grain for a neighbor. Jennings, Rolla, and Wayne had just arrived home from working somewhere else. Merl, Perry, and Clarence were busy hauling manure. And Ruby was churning butter. And they were about to enjoy fried chicken for dinner, their second time. Farm families looked forward to their chickens getting large enough to fry.

Donald Wilson was born September 14, with his Grandmother Laura there to assist both Leora and the doctor. It was an election year, 1916, so they waited until after the vote to give him a middle name.

The Goffs must have bought one of those "$50 on up" pianos from Dowd's in Guthrie Center. Georgia Goff's October letter reported that Merl and Ruby were playing the song "Memories" as a duet, with Merl on violin and Ruby at the piano.

President Woodrow Wilson was reelected, which gave baby Donald a middle name, Woodrow. President Wilson's slogan was "He Kept Us Out of War."

Mattie Simmons Black, Pa's first cousin and the mother of those three children who died during the summer, had another child on November 24. They named her Therma Rosalyn.

The Wilson family spent Thanksgiving Day, November 30, with the Goff clan at Wichita.

Sherd and Laura, Georgia, [unknown], Leora and Clabe with Delbert, and Rolla Goff, November 1916

The Wilsons were also at Wichita in December 1916.

Clabe with Delbert, then Leora holding Donald. The only others identified are Ruby in white, then Laura and Sherd. December 1916, maybe Christmas, Wichita

CHAPTER 38

The Great War, Clabe's Mother Unwell (1917)

In January 1917, Clabe's widowed mother, who lived at Panora with two young daughters, had four teeth pulled under local anesthesia by Dr. E. R. Swank in Panora. (Total charge was $4.00.)

The Guthrie Times announced February 1, that Sherd Goff "made a business trip to Stuart last week. He owns part of the former Adventist College farm east of Stuart. We are told that in the spring that Sherd and family will move to the Stuart place. He had sold his fine Wichita place to the boys." Those boys were his oldest sons.

Leora, at 27, was the only one of the Goff children married. The others were Merl (25), Wayne (24), Georgia (23), Jennings (21), Rolla (19), Ruby (17), Willis (15), Perry (13), and Clarence (11).

Hoping to starve Britain and France into submission, Germany announced unrestricted submarine warfare against neutral and merchant vessels. The United States was outraged, but still resisted going to war, even though they lost three merchantmen in March.

Not knowing when or whether Clabe would be called up by the draft board, the Wilsons sold all their stock, machinery, and some household goods. They moved to a weathered farmhouse on three acres of land near Glendon. Leora set about to make the house a home.

Glendon was on the *Liza Jane* railroad branch line to Guthrie Center from Menlo, and at one time had a church, a store, a blacksmith, and even a hotel with a restaurant.

Clabe went to work for the Glendon Brick and Tile Works, which manufactured tile brick and blocks. He bought his first car, a Model T Ford, second-hand from a neighbor, for some $400.

The US declared war on Germany April 6. Selective Service for men ages 21-39 began in May for what was called the Great War, or even the War to End All Wars. Clabe Wilson's name was among those subject for the draft, as well as three of Leora's brothers—Merl, Wayne, and Jennings.

Nevertheless, both Merl and Jennings bought Kissel Kars.

Clabe Wilson at the Glendon Brick and Tile Works, 1917

Jennings Goff's Kissel Kar (note the Kissel pennant at right): L-R: Jennings, Clabe with Donald, Leora, Delbert is with Perry Goff, May 20, 1917, Wichita

Clabe's mother had some kind of "attack" during the summer. Her daughter, Fonnie, age 14, stayed with her older sister, Alice McLuen of Stuart, who had three small children.

The youngest sister, Verna, lived with Clabe and Leora. She attended school in Glendon, singing as she walked home, with compass plants, cattails, and bull thistles lining the road.

One day the place was so quiet that she and Leora wondered what those little boys were up to. They hunted outside and found them in the machine shed with a mother cat and her kittens. Donald accidentally sat on one of the kittens. Instead of standing up when it meowed, he tried to pull it out. Leora returned the kitten to its nest and found a better place for the boys to play.

Verna with Donald and Delbert, Glendon

Clabe visited his seriously ill mother at least twice in July and paid a total of $160 to the doctor. He paid Dr. J. W. Harrison nearly $80 for his mother's earlier surgery and one-month stay at his private Guthrie Center hospital.

The Exemption Board for the Draft called Clabe for an exam. The whole family rode the *Liza Jane* to Menlo where physicals were set up. He was declared exempt because of his dependent wife and two small children.

At the depot, they watched a troop train heading west on the mainline from Menlo. Leora said it seemed sad to watch that train disappear. "Some of those young men never returned."

August 3, 1917, Guthrie County. Clabe with Donald, Leora, Delbert

CHAPTER 39

Death of Clabe's Mother

Because of all of Georgia Wilson's health problems, Dr. Harrison thought she might do better at The Retreat, a private mental hospital in Des Moines. She could get treatment and also have her daughters with her.

The main building at 28th and Woodland Avenue had been the mansion of James Callanan, an early Des Moines capitalist who was involved with insurance and real estate. An article published in 1904, shortly after his death, said "James Callanan, the late millionaire philanthropist, left his home for drunkards' wives and widows."

Dr. Gershom Hill and Dr. John Doolittle, both having been in charge of the state hospital at Independence, started what was sometimes called Hill's Retreat in 1905. They believed that being able to live in home-like surroundings helped those with nervous and mental disorders. Patients not needing hospital care lived in five cottages, with nurses on duty. A mother could keep her children, and they were allowed to roam the 17-acre grounds, where gardeners tended the orchards and vegetable gardens that supplied the institution.

Informational booklet about The Retreat

But by October, Georgia Wilson was worse. A month later she was admitted to the Clarinda State Hospital, where her husband had died eight years earlier. A legal guardian was named for Fonnie and Verna.

Verna (about 10) and Fonnie (about 14)

Described as 5 feet 7 inches tall, 94 pounds, blue eyes and grey hair, Mrs. Wilson, age 52, was given "baths, massages, medicines and much of the time artificial feeding with no improvement." Depressed and afraid, she worried that someone was trying to break in and worried about business matters. She thought she'd never get well, that nurses and others wanted to torture her. The paranoid woman stayed in bed much of the time.

Georgia Wilson wouldn't respond to questions, nor notice things going on around her. She died there November 25.

After a service for her at the Morrisburg church, Clabe's mother was buried in the nearby Morrisburg Cemetery, with her ancestors instead of with the Wilsons at Coon Rapids.

That says a lot about the undercurrents the family had lived with for years.

CHAPTER 40

Three Goff Brothers Drafted (1918)

In the fall of 1917, Pa and Pa took off for Montana, where his brother Ed Goff and Grandmother Florence lived. Mamma wrote to Leora urging her to "go up and stay a night with the children while we are gone," those "children" ranging in age from 11 to 22.

Evidently, Pa bought a ranch there, but not near Ed and Florence. He put in a crop of winter wheat and spent long hours in the field. Mamma was so used to being surrounded by the hubbub of family; it was too quiet there. She said all she could hear was "the noise of an old bird." She tried singing to herself but became depressed anyway. Pa finally took her to the depot to return to Iowa alone.

President Wilson outlined a Fourteen-Point Program for world peace in early 1918. And the government decreed that each bushel of wheat must make 15 percent more flour, by adding "shorts" and bran, producing flour that was darker and grayish-colored. "We will get used to it."

Clabe submitted a claim against his mother's estate, in order to be reimbursed bills he'd paid to Dr. J. W. Harrison for her surgery, months spent at The Retreat in Des Moines, and days of work lost at the brick plant, totaling $690. At some point, his brother-in-law Ed McLuen objected, stating that Clabe had neglected his mother. Never one to contest anything, Clabe withdrew his claim.

That March, those optimistic Goff boys bought "the Powell ranch on Beaver Creek" and began planting a crop, mostly popcorn. Two months later their draft notices ordered them to report to Camp Dodge.

Jennings, who had bought a Kissel Kar the year before, "put it to good use" the day before leaving home. Then he asked Pa, who was back in Iowa, to sell it for him, which he did. For $1100.

Perhaps a sendoff for the draftees. Wichita, May 26, 1918. Wayne Goff is in uniform, second row, second from the left. His sister Georgia stands in the middle in white Ruby Goff on the right. No one else identified.

But on their Baker Township farm, young corn plants were sprouted. Clabe sold his own acreage and moved to the Goff brothers' place in June to take care of the crops and livestock there. At the somewhat isolated farm, bluebirds darted in the dense nearby thicket. Shy catbirds mewed. Delbert and Donald were small then, and Leora expected another baby later in the summer.

Clabe's sister Verna lived with them, but their sister Rectha, who had moved to Colorado the winter before, asked Verna to stay with her. She decided to go, so Rectha sent her a train ticket.

The 88th Division had been organized at Camp Dodge, north of Des Moines, in September 1917. Men from Minnesota, the Dakotas, Illinois, and Iowa trained there. In April 1918, fifteen recruits died at Camp Dodge from what they thought was a "virulent pneumonia."

Training took about eight weeks–drilling, vaccinations, KP duty, musketry, heavy machine guns, grenade warfare, bayonet combat, automatic arms, gas defense, trench mortar, etc. Temperatures in Iowa reached 100 degrees.

The 88th Division of American Expeditionary Forces (AEF) was activated for combat July 22. Merl and Jennings shipped out with their units on the 31st. Their sisters, Georgia and Ruby, drove to the camp with friends the day before to see them off. Pa arrived the next morning, but he missed seeing Merl. His unit had left on the train at 8:00 that morning. Jennings didn't leave until 2:30 that afternoon, so his father wished him well and also got to watch Wayne on a drill field at gun practice. Wayne didn't leave until August 7.

Mamma refused to see them off at Camp Dodge. Jennings wrote his sister, "If there was anything I could do to keep her from worrying so, I would do it. There is no use to worry. What is to be will be."

On July 30, 1918, Leora wrote her first letter to someone in military service, her brother Jennings. She wrote dozens and dozens of them during two world wars, to brothers and sons in the service.

Merl Goff - AEF 88th Division, 349th Infantry, Co. A. Wayne Goff - 88th Division, 35lst Infantry, Co. M. Jennings Goff - 88th Division, 349th Infantry, Co. K.

Merl and Jennings spent about a week at Camp Upton on Long Island. Jennings asked Leora how the crops were. The Red Cross had given them candy and packaged cigarettes called "Tailor Mades" (already rolled) at a couple of stops.

He didn't suppose they'd get to see Wayne until they were in France, or until "we get back from the big Circus." Temperatures in August reached over 100 degrees across the country. Jennings said it had been so hot that seven people died in New York from the heat.

"They give us wool overcoats, wrapped leggings and a little dink hat without a bill, the steel helmet fits over it." Jennings said that it sounded like the soldiers were hitting the Germans hard, but he thought it would still be a good while before the war was over. "I expect to be in it."

War and record heat and that "virulent pneumonia" at Camp Dodge were more than enough for the Goffs and the Wilsons to worry about.

CHAPTER 41

Doris Wilson Born (1918)

Doris Laurayne was born Friday, August 30 on her uncles' popcorn farm. Grandmother Laura was there to welcome her first granddaughter. "We had her named months before," Leora said, "as I had seemed to believe it was a girl–just had that feeling. Dr. Thomas says, 'How did you know?' I just did." Dr. E. I. Thomas also gave physicals for boys being drafted.

Leora had a batch of bread stirred up and "set" the evening before, to bake the next morning. Her mother baked the bread, making rolls from some of the dough. When little Delbert and Donald came in from playing, they sniffed the warm yeasty aroma. Of course, they each wanted a roll. Then they both wanted another one.

"Oh, if you eat it up all, your Daddy won't have any when he gets home."

Donald, age two, said, "He can eat con-bread," meaning cornbread. Food was rationed during the war, and flour was stretched by adding other grains. Bread made that way didn't keep long, it soured quickly and was sticky. The government encouraged replacing wheat bread with cornbread.

In fact, "An Appeal to the People," by Herbert Hoover of the United States Food Administration, was published in local papers throughout the nation, encouraging eating less in general.

"But the situation with regard to wheat is the most serious in the food supply of the Allied world. . . consumption . . . must be reduced to approximately one-third of normal."

He stressed that "it is imperative that all those whose circumstances permit shall abstain from wheat and wheat products in any form until the next harvest."

The newspaper included a list of substitutes for one cup of wheat flour:

barley 1 ¾ cup
buckwheat ⅞ cup
corn flour 1 scant cup
corn meal, coarse ⅞ cup
corn meal, fine one scant cup
corn starch ¾ cup
rice flour ⅞ cup
rolled oats 1 ½ cup
rolled oats ground in meat chopper 1 ½ cup
soybean flour ⅞ cup
sweet potato flour 1 ½ cup

"This table will help you to make good griddle cakes, muffins, cakes, cookies, drop biscuit, and nut or raisin bread without using any wheat flour."

———————

Rice and Barley Muffins
1 egg
1 cup of milk
1 tablespoon fat
2 tablespoons syrup
4 teaspoons baking powder level
1 teaspoon salt
1 cup rice flour
1 ½ cup barley flour

"Beat egg, add milk, fat and syrup, combine with sifted dry ingredients, bake 20 to 30 minutes in hot oven. These are very delicious."

―――――

Delbert and Donald asked their grandmother if they could take the new baby for a ride in their wagon. "Let's ask your mamma." They tiptoed into the bedroom, where the little boys bumped up against the bed to ask their question. Leora answered that baby Doris needed to get bigger first, so they went back outside to play.

Donald, Clabe holding Doris, and Delbert, on the back porch at "Bear Creek" farm SW of Guthrie Center, 1918. The contraption on the porch was Leora's hand-cranked washing machine.

When Doris was a few weeks old, the popcorn was ready to harvest. Ruby came to help feed the six extra men, including a couple of brothers, Rolla (19) and Willis (16). So they could "board and sleep" the extras, they set up two beds in the front room.

Such a busy time, cooking, scrubbing all those pots and pans, plus nursing the baby. They just couldn't keep the flies out. Leora enclosed the baby's "cab" with netting.

From France, Leora's brothers wrote, "Expect you will be cooking for corn shuckers." "Suppose you're ready to start picking popcorn." "Suppose popcorn is the order of the day."

"Roll Daws has been up to Wichita husking popcorn for Sherd Goff. . ." reported *The Guthrie Times*. "Mr. Goff raised about 2300 bushels this year. The yield was cut short by the hot dry season. About 23 bushels per acre was the average yield. We are told that Sherd has an offer of seven cents per pound for his corn in the ear, 70 pounds per bushels, but will hold for eight cents.

"This would make $5.60 the bushel, or 128.80 per acre. As before stated this has been a lean year. Mr. Goff has raised as much as 50 bushels per acre. Still there are people who say that Iowa corn land is not worth the present selling price. The war is now over and $300 land will be common."

After theirs was harvested, Clabe helped pick corn where it was too far for him to drive back and forth. Certainly capable of taking care of things at home, Leora stayed alone about a week with the baby and two little boys. It was scary at night, in such an isolated place, so the courageous young woman did the evening chores early. A screech owl's hoots and twitters, normally delightful sounds to her, felt eerie. She took the boys with her when she milked two cows, fed the pigs and chickens, and made sure they were in the house with the door locked before it got dark.

One night the cows weren't in from the cornstalk field, so Leora hiked up a hill after them. They didn't respond to her calls. She told the boys to stand by the gate and to stay away from the ditch. By the time she rounded up the cows, Delbert was alone and hollering. Leora rushed down that hill to find Donald climbing out of a ditch, wet and cold. She carried him to the house for a warm bath and put him to bed. Taking Delbert with her to finish the chores, they found the cows by the gate, waiting to be fed and milked.

When Delbert and his mother returned to the house, all was well. Cicadas rasped and treefrogs droned outside, but they were safely locked inside.

When Clabe came home to check on them, he heard Leora's ordeal and decided not to help finish the corn picking. He was needed at home.

Leora was the only married Goff sibling. Her brother Wayne was especially delighted with the news of the birth of his first niece. He sent money home, requesting his sisters buy a gift for the baby. Georgia and Ruby chose a locket, large enough for her to enjoy wearing as an adult. They had it engraved "Wayne to Doris."

Donald, Delbert, and Doris Wilson, 1919

CHAPTER 42

Influenza and the Armistice (1918)

The Guthrie Times often carried news about the local boys serving overseas, even printing letters they'd sent home. It also announced the sad news that Omar Shearer, one of the first to enlist, was the first casualty of the Great War from Guthrie Center.

Red Cross Notes: "A call has come for the collection of old clothes for Belgian Relief. Anything will be acceptable just so it is clean, strong and durable. Shoes are also wanted, in all sizes, scraps of canton flannel to make garments for new born babies. Bring in anything you have within the next ten days and leave in the show room of the Moore Garage . . .

"Also an urgent call has come for the collection of fruit stones, fruit pits and nut shells to be used in making carbon for the protection of our soldiers against the German gas shells. Please have them clean and dry and bring them at once to the Red Cross rooms, where they will be shipped."

The Goff brothers' 88th Division, as support and reserve, participated in the one-million-man Meuse-Argonne campaign. By then, wide-spread influenza had set in among soldiers of the 88th. In eight days there were 1370 cases in one regiment alone, and eighty deaths just on October 14. In all, they lost a total of 444 soldiers from influenza and pneumonia. None of this was revealed until after the war.

Soldiers' letters were censored, and the Goff brothers did not breathe a word about any serious illness.

Back at Camp Dodge, the base hospital was quarantined, then all of the camp itself, with 500 cases of influenza. Newspapers carried advice from the Surgeon General on how to evade the disease: "avoid needless crowding, smother your coughs and sneezes, choose and chew your food well, wash your hands before eating. Seek to make nature your ally not your prisoner by avoiding tight clothes, tight shoes, or tight gloves."

Vicks VapoRub ads called the epidemic, "Simply the Old-Fashioned Grip Masquerading Under a New Name." People hung camphor balls and garlic around their necks. Others gargled with disinfectants. A shoe store said that "One way to keep the flu away is to keep your feet dry."

By October, public funerals were prohibited by the state board of health. Camp Dodge was inundated with more than 1500 soldiers and others sick with influenza. Fourteen barracks next to the hospital were annexed to house patients. Fort Des Moines was also under quarantine.

The October 5, 1918, *Des Moines Tribune* reported that local hospitals were refusing patients with the flu. Four days later, the Army announced that it would no longer release daily reports on the disease.

Des Moines schools opened long enough to hand out information on fighting the flu, and to send the children home. A general quarantine for the city of Des Moines closed theaters, pool halls and gathering places. Stores shortened the hours they were open.

On November 11, after more than four years of fighting and the loss of life in the millions, the guns on France's Western Front fell silent. The armistice between Germany and the Allies signaled the end of the war.

Jennings Goff had been in action just eleven days, and was ready to return to the front. He wrote that on the 11th month, 11th day and 11th hour the war ended. "I was within sound of the guns when they stopped at 11:00 sharp." He celebrated with a bottle of beer but didn't feel well afterward. He expected to be home before the daisies bloomed again.

Wayne wasn't sent to the front, but Merl was for two days. Merl wrote that he had his "fighting pack rolled Sunday morning and ready for the order to go to the big front. We were close enough to hear the big guns plain. We heard the last shots. We heard the armistice was signed but didn't know whether to believe it or not, till the big noise stopped."

People around the globe reacted with relief, a profound sense of loss, and celebration.

When the Wilsons heard the good news they got dressed for town and drove to Guthrie Center to celebrate, along with people from miles around. "The whistle in town blew while all marched down main or State Street, through the town and back."

Clabe and Pa kept Delbert and Donald corralled while visiting with friends and neighbors. Leora, her sisters, and Mamma took turns carrying 10-week-old Doris.

"It was a very happy time and we stayed 'til late at night. An effigy of the Kaiser was burned," Leora wrote later. A model of the Kaiser was burned in effigy across Europe and the United States. Even in Guthrie Center, Iowa

After the Armistice, the 88th Division started an intensive four-weeks' training program, in case they were called as part of an Army of Occupation. They collected salvage, all traces of more than four years of warfare. Jennings received a letter from an Iowa girl named Tessie. "I understand she is your near neighbor," he told his folks. He supposed that Ruby could play any of the popular songs on the trombone by then.

Sugar was rationed at home, but even after the fighting was over, the soldiers had a hard time finding candy in France. Merl asked his mother to send some of the best candy she could for Christmas, without coconut. He bought some French candy, but he was sick all night after eating it.

Candy is what Jennings wanted, too. He'd grown a mustache, but it must not have lasted very long. His sister needn't be afraid he'd come home with a female hanging on his arm. "One American girl is worth a dozen French," he wrote from Reffroy, France.

Merl, at Trevery, France, had been "up to the front Halloween night, but they didn't pick me off." He thought they should stay overseas until the flu improved in America. Besides, it was more fun over there, he added.

Wayne bought souvenir hankies to send home, plus a silk apron for his first niece.

From *The Guthrian*, December 1918: "At a women's meeting the other day a speaker warned the assembly against the purchase of Hun toys, which she said were coming to this country by the ship load. She advised the audience to look for the manufacturer's stamp, and to buy nothing made in Germany. We doubt if many Hun toys will get here for Christmas, but doubtless many Hun products will seek a market here when trade channels open . . . But if you are particular you look for the made in U.S.A. stamp and then you are sure that you are not fattening the pocket of a baby butcherer. The combination of Wilhelm's Gott and Santa Claus doesn't somehow appeal to civilized folks."

The war was over, but people still harbored hard feelings against Germany.

By the end of December, the Doughboys of the 88th Division still had no idea when they'd be home. Although the troops of the American Expeditionary Force during the war were called "Doughboys," no one knows where the nickname came from.

The Goffs and the Wilsons celebrated Christmas and the New Year knowing their boys were safe and coming home sometime in 1919. Leora and her mother kept up their correspondence with Merl, Wayne, and Jennings.

CHAPTER 43

The Goffs' Victorian Home (1919)

Former President Theodore Roosevelt died on January 6, the day before Clabe Wilson turned 31 years old.

Not long after, Fred Jordan died at age 29, leaving Rectha a widow in Colorado, with three small sons and her little sister, Verna.

The Goff brothers hoped to be home from France in time to farm, but still hadn't heard when they would move to the coast of France. Toward the end of January, the brothers were together for the first time since they left Camp Dodge. Wayne wrote that Merl and Jennings were getting fat. Merl had already said the same about him.

Wayne spent his 25th birthday (February 24) in a mumps ward. The hospital had a full house.

The 88th Division organized football, basketball, baseball, and track teams, and arranged for boxing, wrestling, and track meets. Jennings took a signal school class for a week at St. Joire, France. Merl had attended a twelve-week school there, and had been to see and hear Miss Margaret Wilson, daughter of President Woodrow Wilson, sing and talk in a large hangar.

Sherd Goff held a sale at Wichita at the end of February, with plans to move to the county seat town of Guthrie Center, population about 1700. He bought Laura probably the house of her dreams—a furnished Victorian.

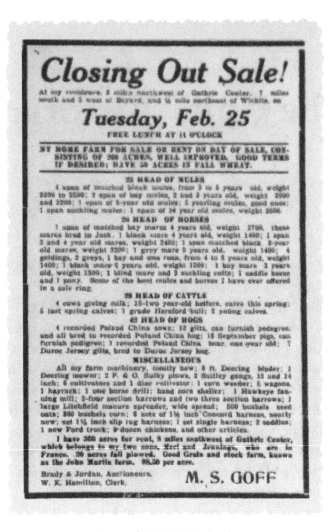

1919 Sale Announcement

With the help of the younger Goffs, they moved their personal belongings. After birthing 11 children, Laura finally got her genteel home, an earthly reward for 13 uprootings in 21 years. The beautiful home came furnished with antiques—a dark oak dining table and buffet with hard-to-dust carvings, a brocade and wicker sofa, and a bedroom set with a four-poster bed. Some of the windows were stained glass.

*Sherd and Laura Goff's Victorian home at
8th and Division Streets in Guthrie Center*

Among other treasures, Laura brought with her the Self-Pronouncing Bible she'd bought when they lived in Minnesota, with her sons' military numbers written in the front, her mother's vinegar cruet and small poppy plate.

Sherd bought a stainless steel popcorn machine, with a round kettle and a crank, so he and his sons could sell his famous popcorn at Guthrie Center events.

Willis, Perry, and Clarence Goff were finally allowed to go to high school. Perry dropped out as a sophomore, shortly after he'd had an appendicitis attack. Sherd kicked him out of the house. Perry worked late at Cronk's Cafe and it was hard for him to get up in the morning. Sherd kicked all the boys out of the house at one time or another.

He had overextended credit to buy farm land, so ended up "going bust" again during the slump in farm prices after the war. His younger sons did get to go to high school, but the older siblings never did get their "cash." He was a hard worker, but he was also a gambler and a horse-trader. His dreams never quite materialized.

CHAPTER 44

A Move to Stuart, Doughboys Come Home

Leora and Clabe relocated to a three-story stucco house on Sherd's farm at Stuart. On the east side of town, it had been part of an Adventist Academy until 1911. Blackboards still hung on the walls in some of the rooms.

The stucco house at Stuart, with family members on the porch

Stuart, in the southeast part of the county, was about the same size as Guthrie Center. The Great White Way, also called U.S. Highway 6 or White Pole Road, connected it to Des Moines to the east, and Omaha to the west, with bands of white paint on the telephone poles to mark the popular route. Situated along the Rock Island Railroad, the town boasted a roundhouse and railroad shops.

Stuart was the terminal for the *Liza Jane* branch train to Guthrie Center, making it handy even for the women in the family to travel back and forth.

The 88th Division was ordered in mid-April to restore the area to its original condition as much as possible, in preparation for the trip home.

Among the first to leave France, Merl and Jennings sailed aboard the USS *Rijndam* at the end of May. Jennings was never so sick in his life. Wayne returned with his unit on the USS *Mercury*, a former German liner, interned by the U.S. in 1917 and converted to a troop carrier.

From the East Coast, they traveled by troop train to Des Moines, where a reception committee met them. The soldiers formed into squads and paraded from the railroad yards to Grand Avenue where they found a big meal provided by various welfare societies. Wayne and Merl were discharged at Camp Dodge in June, Jennings in mid-July.

---o---

THREE SONS IN 88th

Mr. and Mrs M. S. Goff have three sons in the 88th Division. Thursday evening they went to Des Moines, hoping to meet one or all of them. They were fortunate enough to be right there to see their son Wayne get off the train, but Jennings and Merl were detained in Camp Merritt, and Mills but will probably be in this week. Wayne arrived home, Saturday night.

Probably from The Guthrie News, 1919

Wayne Goff with nephews Delbert and Donald

Even before his sons were home, Sherd Goff was on his way to Harlow[ton], Montana, reported the Guthrie Center paper, "near which place he has a large ranch." One of the brothers had mentioned a "half section in Montana," or 320 acres. Harlowton is in the middle of Montana, nowhere near Miles City, where his brother and mother lived. No wonder Laura had felt so isolated there.

The Stuart News, November 13, 1919: "Sunday rained all day. Mon. was a wild, delirious autumn day. Wed. snowed a powder of dry snow with a bitter wind. But, Tue. was a perfect day for Armistice Day Celebration. All roads led to Stuart." Streets in Stuart, still unpaved, were filled with parked cars. Flags floated gaily, with a Fourth of July atmosphere. The band led the parade, followed by members of the GAR post (Grand Army of the Republic, Union veterans of the Civil War), the American Legion (which had been initiated by Lieutenant Colonel Theodore Roosevelt Jr. earlier that year), Boy Scouts, students and their teachers. Two thousand people gathered around the flagpole at Nassau and Division Streets, the children sang, "Iowa" and, of all things, "Marching Through Georgia." Free dinner was served at the Community Building–barbeque beef in buns, pie, doughnuts, pickles and coffee.

Judge McHenry of Des Moines spoke, then Stuart and Panora played a football game, Panora winning 13-0. The Committee paid for movies at the Princess Theater. There was more singing by school children at the Community Building, then a dance to close the day of celebration.

Merl and Jennings had joined the American Legion. But instead of returning to farming, they decided to purchase the Oxford Cafe from F. E. Jordan in Guthrie Center. The newspaper reported that "the boys are now serving the public in the most approved style."

CHAPTER 45

The Influenza
Pandemic, Stuart

The influenza pandemic still lingered after World War I. By the time Clabe and Leora moved to Stuart, she probably thought she'd escaped it. Clabe had endured it a year earlier.

The couple looked forward to celebrating Christmas in Guthrie Center, with her brothers reliving their experiences in France, and vigorous family discussions about politics. Nothing short of a disaster could keep them from bundling up their three little ones, boarding the *Liza Jane*, enjoying winter scenery up the Raccoon River Valley, through Windy Gap near Monteith, and on to the bluffs of the county seat. But Leora came down with the flu just before the Christmas of 1919.

On Christmas Eve, when they heard *Liza's* whistle, one of the Goff boys hiked down to the Guthrie Center depot. The Wilsons weren't on the train. Nor the next morning.

The Wilsons had no phone, so Mamma sent them a poignant postcard: "Willis met the train last night and this morn when Liza whistled, thought sure she was bringing 5 of our very nearest relatives, but we had to give it up."

Decades later Leora remembered: "We had flu the winter of 1919 and 1920—Delbert and Doris didn't have it so bad, but Donald was a sick little boy. . . . I was much sicker than when [Clabe] had the flu in 1918. I got able to write and wrote the folks at Guthrie

155

Center. We were getting over the flu but I was still in bed, doctor's orders, and in a day or so my mother came down to Stuart from Guthrie Center on the Liza Jane train.

"It was after dark, icy, and she had crawled part way, pushing her suitcase along. When I saw her, I couldn't believe my eyes, it seemed so impossible, she came to take care of me and my family. Bless her. She had taken care of my sister and brothers who had flu. She and Pa didn't take flu, a God's blessing."

Leora had survived the deadliest plague in history according to John M. Barry in *The Great Influenza Pandemic*. Before finally fading away in 1920, the virus had prowled around the globe, killing more than 20 million people, even more than the bubonic plague.

Fever was among the first symptoms, then a wracking cough. Victims experienced dizziness, vomiting, sweating, achy joints, trouble breathing. Often, pneumonia set in, overwhelming the sufferer's ears, sinus, and lungs. Death usually came quickly.

More than 500,000 Americans died—6500 in Iowa—dropping our life expectancy a whopping ten years because young adults seemed especially susceptible to complications.

Children recovered, but their young, strong parents would not. Young adults have the strongest, most effective immune systems. But according to Barry, especially at the beginning, the virus was often so efficient at invading the lungs that what had killed young adults, and orphaned so many children, was not the virus itself but the massive response of their healthy immune systems.

The later the virus struck in an area, sufferers weren't as sick, and not as likely to die.

Leora's mother stayed with them several weeks, but Leora, age 29, did not regain her strength until late summer. Even a year later, those who had survived the flu said they still didn't feel right or enjoy their normal energy.

American Legion Day was January 8. Guthrie County Legionnaires celebrated with an oyster supper at the Goff Brothers Cafe.

Leora still wasn't back to normal when the Wilsons moved again to a farm north of Stuart. Before they were out of the three-story house, Mr. and Mrs. Ripley moved in with them. The Ripleys' own children were nearly grown so they enjoyed the Wilsons' little ones. Mr. Ripley held Doris on his lap at mealtime and allowed her to poke her finger in the butter.

As late as April, *The Guthrian* noted that "Mrs. Wilson is just convalescing from a severe attack of flu." She remembered being ready to die, except that she had three small children to care for. And perhaps another on the way.

She must have experienced a flu-related miscarriage. Pregnant women were more likely to die from the flu. And that about a quarter of them who survived lost the baby.

A clue to a July miscarriage comes from a postcard to Leora from her mother: "Sorry you were sick. Take good care of yourself." Another from her sister: "You'll just have to quit working too hard."

CHAPTER 46

Nineteenth Amendment

The Goff Brothers' Cafe didn't last long. They sold it to Frank Cronk after only five months.

Georgia and Ruby started taking music courses that summer at Des Moines College in the Highland Park area of Iowa's capital city. Was their father making it up to them for not allowing them to complete high school? The sisters rode the train back and forth, stopping in Stuart to see their oldest sister's family.

Jennings Goff married Tessie Sauvago, whom he'd mentioned to his folks while he was in France.

In spite of Leora's struggle to return to full health, the Wilsons put in a big garden. Potatoes and Table Queen squash grew in such abundance that they sold their surplus to a Stuart cafe.

"Sent you some parsley," Mamma wrote in October. "Wish you had a whole row of it. Miss Grissell speaks at Christian church tomorrow at 2-30—and tells the women how to vote. think I will learn how its done."

Laura's postcard, October 19, 1920

Just who was Miss Grisell? An aggressive suffragette? Hardly. She had been a Guthrie Center primary school teacher and, in 1909, was secretary of the State Teachers Association.

But by 1920, Blanche A. Grisell was the Guthrie County Recorder. Even though she'd run for office and been elected, it was her first time to vote in an election, and a presidential one at that.

This was the first election after the Great War, and the first after ratification of the 19th Amendment to the Constitution, granting women the right to vote. At 2:30 on that October 20 afternoon she gave a talk about voting to a meeting of the WCTU (Women's Christian Temperance Union) at the Christian Church in Guthrie Center.

The outcome of the first election in which American women voted, including Laura Goff, was that Republican Warren G. Harding won the presidency in a landslide victory.

CHAPTER 47

House Fire,
Another Move (1921)

The Wilsons held a closing out sale before moving into town.

1921 Sale Announcement

Ruby Goff helped them move, but then returned to Des Moines. Clabe took Delbert and Donald with him to look at cows while Leora, seven months pregnant, tore off old wallpaper and burned it in the heater stove and kitchen range. It was a windy early March day but not very cold.

A neighbor man knocked on the door. "Lady, I think your house is on fire!"

Leora carted Doris and a small rocking chair out into the yard and told her to stay there. She did, until a neighbor took her to his place.

Soon firemen arrived while neighbors helped tote everything outside. Leora threw things out the kitchen window, including a clock, which "flew all apart." When Clabe and the boys got home, they found all their belongings in the yard.

The Ripleys, who had moved in with them before they were out of the stucco house, asked them to stay with them until Clabe could find another place. He found one the next day, the Chittick house on Gaines Street.

The Stuart Herald, March 4, 1921: "Fire Destroys Residence. A fire Wednesday afternoon destroyed the former W. E. Delaney home in the extreme north part of town . . . was occupied by Clabe Wilson. Mr. Wilson had just gotten his goods moved into the house when the fire was discovered in the attic, caused by a defective chimney. The roof was soon ablaze and most of the house burned before the fire was put out . . ." Weak water pressure in that part of town made things worse.

There was considerable talk of forming a vigilance committee, since "other towns in the state have organized along this line." From the same issue of *the* Stuart paper, "Now that the roads are good, it would be easily possible for some of the band of robbers who seem to have their headquarters in Des Moines, to come here in the night, commit a robbery and be back in Des Moines before morning."

The March 11 sale bill began: "Our house having burned down, I am forced to move where I cannot keep the following property," including the Jake Blackman mules, Poland China brood sows (pedigreed and bred to farrow in April), and more.

Mrs. Knox, widowed in November when Dr. Knox died, lived next to the Wilsons on Gaines Street. She enjoyed her new neighbors having small children. The Stuart Beattys lived across the street in a two-story house with an attic. Their son Jack was about the age of Delbert and Donald. He had lots of toys and books, and a German Shepherd named Husky.

Jennings and Tessie Goff had a baby girl on March 3, named Maxine. Sherd and Laura Goff now had two grandsons and two granddaughters.

CHAPTER 48

Nightwatchman Killed, Clabe is Hired (1921)

The town of Stuart was shocked when would-be bank robbers shot the nightwatchman, John Kerr Myers, age 70, who died the next morning. He'd been their night marshal since 1915. Two of his daughters taught in the Stuart schools, another in Harlan, Iowa.

The Stuart Herald, April 14, 1921:

REWARD FOR BANK ROBBERS AND MURDERERS

"Early Wednesday morning, March 30th, 1921, a bunch of armed yeggmen [safecrackers or burglars] fatally shot Nightwatchman J. K. Myers at Stuart, Iowa, and attempted to burglarize the First National Bank of the same place." Rewards offered: $500 by the State, $500 by the bank, and $1000 by the Guthrie County Bankers' Association.

"The five armed yeggmen who committed the crimes stole a car from in front of the Orpheum Theater, in Des Moines, and made their safe return to that city where the car was found." Signed by C. C. Kennedy, Sheriff, Guthrie County, Iowa.

Yeggmen, as *The Guthrian* called them, had stolen a Hudson six from in front of the Orpheum Theater in Des Moines the night of March 29. In the middle of the night, the five men ordered breakfast at Stuart's Princess Cafe, where train crewmen ate at odd hours. They broke into a shed at the coal chute, stole a pickax, a sledge, and a chisel which they used to break into the Stuart bank.

Mr. Myers, walking through the alley south of the bank at 4:15 a.m., came upon some of the gang, tried to arrest them, and shooting began.

Even though the thugs had cut many nearby phone wires, a woman living in rooms above the harness shop was awakened by the gunshots. Her son rang up "central," the local telephone operator, and soon the town was roused by the fire whistle.

Townsmen took Mr. Myers to the hospital. The robbers didn't get any cash before they were discovered, but one of three bullets that had hit Mr. Myers severed an artery in his leg. He died at 8:30 that morning.

Stuart men formed a posse and notified surrounding towns of the attempted robbery. They also telephoned the sheriffs of Guthrie and Polk Counties as well as the Des Moines police department. A bullet had pierced the radiator of the getaway car. Racing to Des Moines, the criminals stopped at a farm near Earlham for gas, and water for the radiator.

When the black Hudson sped through Van Meter, several men fired shots at it. The car, with bullet holes in it and blood stains on the seats and floor, was found in Des Moines later that morning in a shed in an alley between Locust and Walnut, west of Ninth.

A week later, Clabe Wilson was appointed as the new night-watchman. Their neighbor, Stuart Beatty, suggested he take their German Shepherd, Husky, when on duty. Clabe sent Husky into alleys behind the merchants' shops to sniff around stacks of wooden crates and boxes stored there. Clabe's salary was set at $73.60 per month, by June raised to $85 per month.

Stuart Nightwatchman, Clabe Wilson

Clabe's family watched him walk up the street with Husky, carrying a gun and wearing a star-shaped badge, Leora and three small children, ages two to five. Delbert, nearly six, sensed that his mother was worried. Her twins were due next month.

CHAPTER 49

Arrests, Twins Dale and Darlene Wilson (1921)

The town provided the nightwatchman a .32 caliber revolver, but Clabe didn't trust it. Instead, he carried a sawed-off shotgun with buckshot and a .45 caliber pistol of his own. Clabe held target practice north of town, often taking young sons with him.

Since he worked nights, Clabe slept during the day. With windows open during nice weather, it was hard for Leora to keep her own and neighbor kids from hollering or whacking croquet balls in the yard.

Clabe plowed a spot for a garden using a workhorse. He needed both hands to guide the single-blade plow so he strapped the reins around his waist. It was warm enough that a barefoot Doris followed the furrows. The youngsters were anxious to take off their shoes in the spring, but had to ask permission, first. Robins swooped close to Doris in order to snatch the worms unearthed by the plow.

Clabe hoisted Doris on his shoulders and swung her around. She held onto his hair, laughing, then found a smooth spot on his face with her hands to give him a kiss.

Leora entertained her young ones by marching them around the table while she sang. One ditty was the "Ragpicker Song, "which went, "Any rags, any bottles, any bones today?" Some were Civil War tunes she remembered her own mother singing when she was a child.

On May 12, one man was arrested for the murder of Mr. Myers. The next day Wilsons' twins, Dale and Darlene, were born.

Grandmother Laura was there to help for several days. When she returned to Guthrie Center on the *Liza Jane*, she took three-year-old Doris with her. Decades later Doris still remembered bedding hanging on a clothesline when the train made a stop at Monteith, waking in the Victorian house to her grandmother's low voice, the rich brown smell of coffee boiling, playing in the turreted stairway, and gazing up at the lovely stained glass.

Her aunts Georgia and Ruby doted on Doris, making dresses for her out of some of their own. They'd lift their little niece on the table and slowly turn her to pin the hem in a dress. She slept upstairs, where the oil lamp made eerie shadows on the walls. A flowered pitcher sat in a bowl on a chest of dark wood, like the rest of the furniture.

One day, Grandmother heard Doris crying and found her slumped with her head on her knees on the staircase. "What's wrong, honey?"

"I want my boys," meaning her brothers. She was homesick. Grandmother gathered her onto her lap and soothed her, singing in her low alto voice, "In the Sweet Bye and Bye" and "The Little Brown Church in the Vale."

Grandpa Sherd said he'd buy her a doll, any doll she wanted. Georgia and Ruby took her downtown, and found the biggest and best doll there, wearing a yellow dress. Doris noticed one she liked better, a smaller one dressed in pink. "Let's look at the big one again," her aunts coaxed. "Wouldn't you rather have it?" No, she wanted the pink one.

Sherd had business in Stuart, so he was the one who took Doris home, helping her climb the big steps onto the train car. When they arrived at the Stuart depot, he parked the doll under his arm while helping his granddaughter climb down the steps. As usual, he found someone to gab with, and was soon in conversation with another man. Doris heard a crash, and there was the pink doll, sprawled on the platform with a broken head.

She tugged at Grandpa's coat. "I'll get you another," he promised, but he never did. Doris didn't care. She just wanted to go home.

A second suspect of the murder of Mr. Myers was arrested in July. John Watters and Dave Masters were indicted by a Guthrie County Grand Jury for first degree murder, and for breaking and entering. The State asked for the death penalty. Clabe Wilson attended the trial, riding back and forth on the train. But in spite of over three dozen witnesses for the State at the Guthrie County Courthouse, and after twenty-seven hours of deliberation, the jury acquitted both men.

When young Delbert watched his father go up the street at night, he worried. But he was also proud of him... carrying a gun and wearing a badge. And all the kids at school knew who his dad was.

Clabe came home with a twin baby carriage, which he had to assemble. Leora took the twins in their "double cab buggy" on the train to visit her folks at Guthrie Center. The Victorian house was up a hill to the northeast of the depot, a good hike even without pushing a stroller. But her siblings probably met them at the station.

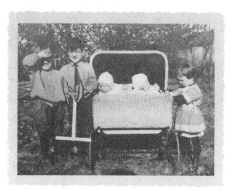

Nov. 6, 1921. L-R: Donald, Delbert, Dale and Darlene in the "double cab buggy," Doris, Stuart

171

Parading uptown to get groceries or the mail in Stuart was a family affair. Leora pushed the twins in the cab. Doris rode in a wagon, with Del and Don pushing and pulling it. On their way home, with the wagon full of groceries, Doris rode on the front of the cab. A woman stopped to see the twins and asked who was the one on the front. "Well, this is the triplet," laughed Leora, but Doris was embarrassed.

Mrs. Knox visited Leora often. "You folks don't need to go out for entertainment," she said. "You have it at home." Aunt Georgia sometimes stayed with them. Once after Delbert, Donald, and Doris had baths in a tin tub with Cuticular soap, Georgia lined them up in Mrs. Knox's old-fashioned ferns for a well-loved photo.

Doris (in blue and white gingham), Donald, and Delbert

CHAPTER 50

Smallpox (1922)

Smallpox was a terrible disease. On average, 3 out of every 10 people who fell victim to it died, according to the CDC. Sufferers who survived usually had scars, sometimes severe.

It's "a contagious, disfiguring and often deadly disease that has affected humans for thousands of years," says the Mayo Clinic website. "Naturally occurring smallpox was wiped out worldwide by 1980—the result of an unprecedented global immunization campaign."

An adult Guthrie Center man died from smallpox, as well as three children, reported the Stuart newspaper in February 1922. A 23-year-old Monteith woman succumbed to it as well. Her father dealt with a milder case because he'd been vaccinated six decades earlier, during the Civil War.

Clabe and Leora quickly took their children for vaccinations. Locals wondered whether the disease had been spread by a neighborhood cat. No wonder people were fearful.

Death at Monteith Due to Smallpox

Guthrie Center, Ia., Feb. 14.—Black smallpox has again broken out here, believed to be carried by one of the cats from the Frank Sturdevant home where Mr. Sturdevant died. First the cat visited the Persons home where it was handled by the little 2-year-old daughter and returned to the Burr home. As a result, over two weeks later, the Persons girl and two of the Burr children became victims of the disease. There is great excitement over the town and doctors' offices are crowded continually with people waiting to be vaccinated.

Florence Morehead, a girl living near Monteith, died a few days ago with black smallpox. She had contracted the disease from her father, an aged man, who had recovered from an attack, but not being sick enough to call a doctor was not aware of the nature of this ailment. He had been vaccinated while serving in the civil war.--Register.

The Stuart Herald, February 17, 1922

Instead of a single injection, the smallpox vaccination was administered on the upper arm with a circle of needle pricks, then the serum was daubed onto the area and covered with a bandage. It caused a blister which eventually fell off, leaving the circular scar as evidence of the vaccination. The vaccinated Wilson children were spared this dreaded illness.

That year the Ku Klux Klan harassed the Catholics in Stuart. Clabe declared them cowards since they hid their faces.

A salesman distributed boxes of Jell-O to each house in Stuart. Leora declared the stuff unfit to eat, something made from pigs' feet. She couldn't use it anyway since they didn't have an ice box. Once or twice a week, the ice wagon made deliveries. Whoever wanted to buy ice posted a sign in their window indicating the amount, 25 pounds or whatever. When the man chipped off the amount and hauled it to a house, neighborhood kids ran to the wagon to steal chips. "You kids get away from there!"

After Leora put the twins to bed, Doris was tucked in next, in a room just off the dining area. Leora left the door ajar so little Doris could hear her reading *Mother Westwind* stories to Delbert and Donald at the round table with an oil lamp aglow. Doris, in the dark room, could picture each character–Sammy Jay, Reddy Fox, Jerry Muskrat, and all the many others.

Come Christmastime, Leora sang "Jolly Old Saint Nicholas" for her youngsters, but substituted their names:

Jolly old Saint Nicholas, lean your ear this way.

Don't you tell a single soul what I'm going to say.

Christmas Eve is coming soon, now you dear old man

Whisper what you'll bring to me. Tell me if you can.

Delbert wants a story book. Doris wants a dolly.

Donald wants some roller skates–he thinks dolls are folly

As for me . . .

CHAPTER 51

Death of Georgia Laurayne Goff (1922)

Des Moines families liked to hire students from Drake University to help with children and housework. The Carl Weeks family, who later built Des Moines's treasured Salisbury House, hired Georgia and Ruby Goff, ages 27 and 21Ruby cooked for them at their home at 1324 39th Street, and Georgia was so good with their sons that she even accompanied the family to vacation at Clear Lake in the summer of 1921.

Carl and Leo Weeks founded the Armand Company, which made cosmetics, around 1915. By 1927, *Fortune* magazine said Armand led the nation in the sale of face powder.

Both sisters took music and other classes, traveling back and forth by train from Des Moines to Stuart and Guthrie Center.

But by the next spring, Ruby wrote home that Georgia was having spells, and they needed to come take her home. Even after that, Georgia had good days and gave piano lessons to several children in Guthrie Center. As the spells worsened, she eventually gave those up, as well as the beau she dated.

When Georgia visited her sister in Stuart, four-year-old Doris felt comfortable with her. Georgia tucked her niece's small hand in her pocket to keep it warm when they walked uptown. Once when a torn spot in the roll for their player piano made a discordant noise, it caused Georgia to make guttural noises. Leora put her arms around her sister, "Oh, Georgia, Georgia, don't." It frightened Doris.

Doris witnessed one of the spells at her grandparents' home in Guthrie Center. Sherd Goff struck his daughter. Grandmother cried, "Oh, Pa Pa, don't."

At his wit's end, Sherd took his daughter to Clarinda Mental Health Center, where she was admitted August 22. "So, Pa, that's where you think I should go." She died only ten days after arriving.

A letter from the Clarinda Treatment Complex noted that Georgia Goff was intelligent and obedient to her parents, a student of music and dramatic art, and also studied "applied psychology by intensive concentration." The reason for admission: "Over study and nervous breakdown." Diagnosis: "Manic Depressive Psychosis: Mania."

Cause of death: "Exhaustion and acute Mania: Congestion of the brain." Her funeral was held in the parlor of the Goff's Victorian home, which was filled with mourners. Georgia was the first of the family buried in Union Cemetery.

GEORGIA L. GOFF (OBITUARY)

"A very sad death which occurred, last Thursday, was that of Miss Georgia Goff, daughter of Mr. and Mrs. M.S. Goff of this city. Her demise was caused from brain fever, and her illness was short.

"Georgia Laurayne Goff was born April 29, 1894 at Bloomfield Knox County, Nebraska, and died September 7, 1922, aged 28 years, four months and eight days. In 1896, she came with her parents to this county to live. Later they moved to Minnesota, returning here in 1905.

"During recent years, Miss Goff has been a resident of Des Moines, working and attending Drake University where she was a student of dramatic art and music. It is thought that it was her close application to work and studies which brought on the illness which caused her death.

"She was a quiet girl of gentle manner and disposition. She had an ambition to excel in everything good and worth while, and never lowered her high ideal although her too frail body could not stand what was required of it.

Georgia Laurayne Goff

"She leaves to mourn her passing, her parents, two sisters, Mrs. Leora Wilson of Stuart, and Miss Ruby Goff, and seven brothers, Merle [sic], Wayne, Jenning[s], Rolla, Willis, Perry and Clarence. One other brother preceded her in death in 1909 . . ."

From *The Guthrie Times*

CHAPTER 52

Danny Wilson Born (1923)

The weather turned warm the first part of March, then a blizzard began in Stuart on Thursday the 15th. The wind switched to the northwest and it snowed the rest of the day, that night, all day Friday, Friday night, and Saturday. By Sunday, snow was piled up higher than fences. The easiest way to get around was on a sled. Townspeople scooped snow from the tracks so the *Liza Jane* could get through.

Grandmother came in May to be with Leora during the birth of another new baby. Daniel Sheridan Wilson, named for both grandfathers, was born in the Chittick house on Gaines Street. Clabe's father was Daniel Ross Wilson. Leora's was Milton Sheridan Goff, but called "Sherd."

Delbert and Donald followed their dad around, and the twins, Dale and Darlene, had just turned two. Now another baby. What to do with four-year-old Doris?

Doris rode home with her grandmother again, to that lovely Victorian home. She was fascinated by a picture on one wall of a girl watching a robin. "Why doesn't the robin fly away?" Doris wanted to know. She hadn't had much luck catching one.

One day, Doris caught one in the yard. She was homesick, so smuggled the robin into bed with her. When Grandmother found her, she was chagrined. "Lawsy, girl. You have mites crawling on you. Let's take the robin outside. You'll have to have a bath." That activity was next.

Willis and Clarence Goff graduated from Guthrie Center High School in 1923. Willis was 21 by then. Clarence, at 17 and the seventh son, was valedictorian of the class. He won a scholarship but the family felt he was too young to go to college. Willis used it instead, studying chemistry at the University of Iowa.

Willis also bummed around, riding the trains. He hopped off the Rock Island line at Stuart once, planning to catch the branch train to Guthrie Center. He lost his balance and fell into a firebox pit between the rails. If it had been a fresh dump, he'd have been scalded. Cold, wet, black, and looking like a tramp, Willis trudged through town to the Wilsons' place. His sister heated water so he could take a bath and gave him some of Clabe's clothes. After having something to eat, he slept a long time. Leora washed his filthy clothes with her hand-powered washer, ringer, and washboard, and pegged them on the clothesline to dry.

One time when the Wilsons visited folks in Guthrie Center, Delbert and Donald trekked south of town a ways to the Raccoon River with Boyd Parrish, son of Laura Goff's youngest sister, Cora. Boyd, about eleven years old, was three years older than Delbert. They could see the river bottom so the boys sloshed in, not realizing they couldn't reach the bottom. The brothers panicked and Donald swallowed some water. Boyd managed to rescue them both.

Clabe had been Stuart's nightwatchman for about two years when he learned that a Dexter man wanted a tenant farmer with a family. B. C. Hemphill offered $60 per month, a hog to butcher, half a beef, the right to raise chickens, free rent, room for a large garden, and even a horse to ride.

Knowing that Leora was all for living on a farm again, where she could raise a flock of chickens, he took the job.

CHAPTER 53

Hemphill Place and Eye Surgery (1923)

The Hemphill place was two or three miles southeast of town, but Mr. Hemphill lived in Dexter. His big house and barn were just east of the school, and north of the Presbyterian church.

The Wilsons moved everything to the farm, including the kitchen sink, which sat in a wooden oilcloth covered table. The porcelain sink was so heavy that Clabe needed help setting it down in the hole cut for it, with a "slop bucket" underneath.

He hung Leora's "Home Sweet Home" and nailed the plate rail to the dining room wall. The shelf held an iridescent orange vase with a fluted top, pretty plates, and a glass hatchet with two gold tassels.

Mr. Hemphill drove his kerosene-burning Model T Ford to the farm and gave the Wilsons a hog. They butchered it that fall and rendered the fat in pans in the oven. They stored it in five and ten-gallon crocks, the same ones used for making sauerkraut. Leora cooked with the lard, making doughnuts right away, a rare aromatic treat.

The two rooms off the kitchen became the pantry and the "bawl room." The room where a crying child was sent had coats and boots on one side, wash tubs on the other. The reservoir and pump on the back porch made it easy to fill the tubs.

They moved just before Doris's August 30th birthday. Dale, Doris,
and Darlene at the Hemphill place. The wash drying
at left, Leora's houseplant starts on the front porch.

Second graders, Delbert and Donald, rode the landlord's gentle
pony to school. Clabe showed them how to bridle Nancy, but he
needed to saddle her each morning. How handy it was to leave
the horse at the landlord's during the day.

Delbert and Donald, just arrived home from school.
Donald's 7th birthday, September 14, 1923, SE of Dexter

Decades later, Leora Wilson wrote, "They did pretty good, even did grocery shopping. I would send a list of groceries to get when they left for school and they would get the groceries after school. Their father fixed a grain sack with a draw-string to hang over the saddle horn. Once they came home and no sack of groceries. They went back and someone had picked the sack of groceries up and hung it on a fencepost—all the groceries were there."

Clabe had finished the morning milking about daybreak in December, closing a gate and fastening it with a wire over a post. The wire sprang up, hitting him in the eye. When he got to the house, his eye was bloody. Leora helped him saddle Nancy. They all watched him ride into a cold north wind to the doctor.

He came home, a patch over the eye, with orders to see a specialist in Des Moines. Leora gathered up things she thought he might need, including his dollar Ingersoll pocket watch. The Rock Island tracks ran just north of the farm on the way to Des Moines. Clabe's family watched and waved as the train headed east to the big city. There he underwent surgery, then had to lie still several days.

He made several trips to Des Moines to have the eye checked and dressed. Leora and the kids always anticipated the train so they could wave, the kids standing atop a haystack. He began leaving Nancy at home, following the railroad track on foot to the depot.

CHAPTER 54

Death of Tessie Goff (1924)

Tessie Goff, Jennings's wife, gave birth to Merrill on January 27, 1924. Both mother and baby came down with mumps. Four days later, Tessie died from it. Mumps is a viral infection affecting salivary glands near the ears, causing fever, headache, and tiredness. Complications are more common in adults than children.

Tessie was buried in the Goff plot at Guthrie Center near Georgia Laurayne Goff, who had died just over a year earlier.

Tessie's folks, the Sauvajos of Wichita, tended baby Merrill while the Goff grandparents kept three-year-old Maxine, who was sick then with measles. Lasting a week or more, measles is also very contagious. Beginning with fever, cough, runny nose, and inflamed eyes, then a rash starts a few days later. Common complications include diarrhea, earache, and pneumonia.

These folks, especially Jennings, must have been overwhelmed with mourning Tessie and tending sick little ones.

At the same time, the Wilson children had caught measles. Delbert and Donald fell ill first, then Doris, then the twins.

Leora fixed milk toast (milk poured over bread cubes, then sprinkled with brown sugar) and carried the comforting treat upstairs to the sufferers. Probably the same remedy her own mother used, it at least soothed young ones. Grandmother Laura prescribed plenty of warm drink, cool water, and to be careful not to catch colds.

That April, Leora bought 200 Rhode Island Red eggs for hatching. A month later, she bought 100 more plus 22 duck eggs.

They bought an incubator with an oil burner, about 4 X 5 feet and on legs, for about 12 dozen eggs. They kept the incubator in the center of the living room. Doris woke up one night and came halfway down the stairs. She watched as her folks turned each brown egg by the light of an oil lamp. How interesting that they were still busy so late.

Leora sent for two Rhode Island Red cockerels, young roosters. Their large combs flopped over oddly and one, trying to take a drink, fell into the horse tank. The kids found it floating. Just in case he might survive, Leora carried the lifeless rooster in an old tub (the one they used to clean rabbits for supper) and placed it behind the cookstove. Doris wondered why her mother had put the dead chicken in the kitchen, but before the sun was up the next morning, they heard crowing downstairs.

One broody hen, ready to sit on a clutch of eggs, arranged her nest under the granary. Leora pulled on a pair of Clabe's overalls over her dress, crawled under, and gathered the eggs.

Salesmen used to go door to door, even farm to farm, to find a housewife home, hoping she'd buy their wares. Once when a magazine salesman came to the Wilson place, Leora had no cash to pay for a magazine. He said he'd take a couple of hens for a subscription. It was a deal.

Spring cleaning began as soon as it was warm enough to take down the heating stove. There was so much more room so Leora rearranged the furniture, aired out the house, washed windows and curtains, and hoisted rugs over the clothesline for the kids to beat out the dust.

Clabe found an ad for a German Shepherd pup. Would they take a revolver in trade? Yes, they would. So Clabe mailed the gun, and the pup arrived on the train. They named him Husky after Beatty's dog in Stuart. Husky was always afraid of storms and guns. He'd shove himself into the house and hide under the big table during a storm. Just leave him alone until the storm is over, Leora told the kids, and he'd be okay. She was Husky's favorite human, probably because she fed him.

During 1924, Leora sold 135 chickens (earning 14 to 18 cents per pound) and 92 dozen eggs (earning 36-47 cents a dozen). Selling eggs and chickens enabled this mother of six youngsters to order a brand new Singer sewing machine through the Sears, Roebuck catalog. The mailman left a note that a package, which was too large to come on the route, had arrived at the post office. Leora waited for the boys to get home from school, hitched Nancy to a buggy, then drove back to town to get her treasure.

She powered the handy machine by rocking the treadle back and forth with her feet, sewing and repairing clothing, bedding, and curtains. Leora worked on her sewing projects while the big kids were at school and the little ones napped.

CHAPTER 55

Clabe Bobs His Wife's Hair

Leora read the Sunday paper aloud to her family. Clabe's bad eye still bothered him and he enjoyed hearing her read. So did the kids, especially when she read the funny papers. Clabe became so tickled, he'd almost cry.

The "shingle bob" for women was introduced about 1923, very short in the back, exposing the hairline at the neck. Leora found a picture she liked in a newspaper of a woman with bobbed hair. It may have given directions about how to go about accomplishing it. Leora could trim her daughters' hair that way, but not her own.

"Clabe, I want you to cut my hair this way. We'll use this picture and I'll guide you."

Leora's hair was dark brown and thick. She'd worn it long ever since childhood. Clabe admired Leora's mass of dark brown hair, so he took a very long time to make that first cut. Leora kept encouraging him, with all the kids watching. Each snip was probably nerve wracking for him. Afterward he said, "A person ought to be kicked for doing a trick like this."

The Christmas before their wedding, he'd given her a silver vanity set—mirror, brush, and comb. The mirror and comb were most likely part of this historic hair bob.

Chores for Del and Don included shelling and cracking corn for the chickens and keeping the stock tank pumped full of water.

They told Doris that if you put a horsehair in a rain barrel, it would someday turn into a snake.

Leora strained insects from the soft water for hair-washing and for watering her houseplants. Neighbors exchanged plant slips with each other, and the window box she could see just outside the kitchen overflowed with vines.

Delbert and Donald often explored with Husky, sometimes along the railroad tracks. One exciting day, Husky chased an animal into a culvert. He barked at one end while the boys squatted at the other to watch. The critter whistled at them. They finally gave up and hiked home, announcing they'd found a new animal.

Clabe asked them to describe it. "Well, it's not a new animal. You found a groundhog. They like to live under things, like a shed. Show me where you found him and we'll take a look at the tracks."

Sure enough, they found imprints with four toes in front and five on the back. They also found Husky's tracks and where their pet had scuffled with excitement at one end of the culvert.

Clabe was more comfortable observing people than carrying on a conversation. When a neighbor came to visit, he was shyer than with family. But he knew native animals and their habits.

He taught his older sons to trap gophers and groundhogs. The landlord paid them 10 cents for gophers and 25 cents for groundhogs, since both could be menaces on a farm. That paid for more traps and some school clothes.

After finishing their chores, the boys were free to explore with Husky. They fished for bullheads in the creek to the south. Howard Benz lived a mile south but went to country school. The three boys fished together and tried catching ground squirrels with lassos. When Delbert and Donald asked their mother to keep Doris from tagging along, she was heart broken.

Doris felt so loved and comforted when her mother wrapped her in a blanket and carried her downstairs. They sat in the rocking chair by the furnace, a rare blessing. Leora usually asked her to go upstairs to see if the younger ones had awakened from napping, and to help them down the steep steps.

Leora, Darlene, and Doris with new hairbobs

Another treat was when Leora gave her daughters shingle bobs, just like they'd watched their dad do for their mother.

CHAPTER 56

The Wilson School Bus (1924)

Sherd and Laura Goff secured a loan on a house in Dexter along White Pole Road. Moving with them were their daughter Ruby, sons Merl and Jennings, and Jennings's motherless children, Maxine and Merrill.

Having her folks so close was one of Leora's fondest hopes. The other was a home of their own but being able to live in the country was a blessing in itself. She was glad her youngsters would have cousins to play with.

When Doris started school, Clabe taught nine-year-old Delbert to hitch Nancy to a rig and drive the "Wilson school bus." They practiced on country roads and around in the farmyard. Doris rode to school between her brothers. Since they left Nancy and the buggy at the landlord's, from time to time, Clabe and the boys cleaned out Mr. Hemphill's barn in town.

Nancy was ready to give Delbert, Doris, and Donald a ride to school in the "Wilson school bus."

Every morning when Leora brushed Doris's fly-away hair before school, she smelled like graham pancakes. Her square one-burner griddle with molds on half of it made four-inch square pancakes. It was hinged for flipping it over to cook the other side. Made with coarse-ground wheat flour, graham pancakes were Clabe's favorite, with cream and brown sugar syrup, but the kids liked big round ones fried in skillets on the back of the stove. They'd "finger over" whichever pancake they claimed so no one else got that one. Leora also made them shaped like a bunny, or a letter of the alphabet.

A bluebird flew ahead of the buggy one time, from fencepost to post, for about a mile, on their way to town. Iowa's autumn roadsides glowed with black-eyed Susans, blue asters, and purple prairie clover. Monarch butterflies visited stalks of milkweed. Dew disclosed gauzy webs of orb-weaver spiders.

One time Husky followed them to school, trotting right up the steps and into Doris's room. The teacher let him lay under her desk, but at recess he jumped up on the sand table and scattered sand. The family thought maybe Husky needed a companion, so they got a rat terrier pup from a neighbor. Clabe took Donald and Doris in the buggy to get it. Trix turned out to be a bossy dog. He loved hunting and when the two dogs came upon a varmint to catch, Husky let Trix catch it. If Husky had something in his mouth, Trix growled until Husky gave it up. The terrier later died after being hit by a car.

Delbert with Trix, Husky, and Donald, January 4, 1925

A mother looks forward to when her children come home after school, even though she often needs to walk one of them through a dilemma. One day, Doris whined that the boys at school made fun of her shoes. "They asked me if they are boys' shoes, and they clomp like boys' shoes." They were still fairly new, but yes, they were ones that Donald had outgrown. I wonder how Leora solved that one.

Then there was the day someone tattled to the teacher that Doris had said a bad word. The teacher asked what she'd said. "I don't know. All I said was 'I'll run like the deuce'." Her brothers always talked like that. The teacher said, "Well, you're too nice a girl to talk like that," and made Doris sit in the cloak room until recess. She cried.

Delbert got in trouble in fourth grade. Doris waited for her brothers, like always because they got out later. Two fourth-grade girls told Doris that he was to be spanked and consoled her. Donald didn't think it was any big deal. Delbert was red-faced when he did come out, wearing a smirk. Leora would have heard that story, as well, but when it came to boys fighting, Clabe gave them a warning.

One of the older brothers fought with a boy at school, ending when the other kid's thumb came out of joint. He'd tucked inside his fist. Clabe cautioned his sons to keep their thumbs outside the fist if they were ever in a fight.

When it snowed one Christmas, Clabe filled the bobsled with hay and hitched up a pair of horses, harnessing them with bells on leather straps. All of the younger bundled-up Wilsons snuggled under quilts with their mother. Delbert, Donald, and Doris stood up front by their dad, who was in charge of the reins. They glided over the snow for Christmas dinner in town with Grandpa and Grandmother, and the rest of the Goff clan, harness bells jangling, horses snorting frosty breaths.

Uncle Clarence Goff had come from Omaha, so there was a good crowd. For the dinner, kids perched on the piano bench, with catalogs to boost up the smaller children. Grandmother served squares of cheese on toothpicks, which was something new and wonderful for the eight grandchildren.

The ninth was due next summer, another Wilson baby.

CHAPTER 57

Life on the Farm

With cousins living in town, the Wilson kids played with them often, sometimes at the farm.

Maxine and Merrill Goff, Doris and Darlene Wilson. January 11, 1925, Dexter

For Easter Sunday, 1925, the three oldest Wilsons wore new duds. Delbert's and Donald's new suits had short pants called knickers, constructed in such a way that the hems could be let out as they grew. Doris wore the soft frock her mother made from light green pongee with shiny figures in the fabric. Her straw hat with cherries came from the Sears, Roebuck catalog. Leora gave her permission to wear the hat to school, but Doris donned it for recess. She loved playing on the giant strides, which were handles hung from a wheel on a tall pole. As kids began to circle the pole, centrifugal force thrust them outwards, especially the smaller ones. While riding the giant strides, she lost the cherries.

Ready for Sunday School on Easter, April 12, 1925.
Delbert, Doris, and Donald. Dexter

One chilly spring evening when the wind had died down, the whole family hiked to the field to burn cornstalks, a task to be done before spring plowing in those days. Delbert and Donald helped rake the stalks into strips to burn. Clabe pulled a hayrake behind two horses. The evening was so quiet, except for the gentle orders to the horses and the snapping of the flames. How good the heat felt in the chill. Doris helped keep the little kids back from the fire.

Neighbors had chosen the same night to burn their stalks. They could see flames across the neighborhood. Red-winged blackbirds added their "che-ree" song to frogs croaking in the distance.

Clabe plowed the big garden north of the house with a horse in early spring. The big kids helped plant the seeds and, as things began to sprout, the family spent evenings in the garden. Clabe showed Delbert and Donald how to hoe carefully while he cultivated.

L-R: Danny, Dale, Darlene, Doris, Donald, and Delbert Wilson. Delbert was dressed up for a birthday picture. June 3, 1925, Delbert's 10th birthday

A barefoot Donald Wilson, age 9, weeding the corn, June 5, 1925

When the family got ready to go to town, Clabe would say, "Leora, put on your lipstick and your babydoll shoes!" She bought the black patent dress shoes with straps and rounded toes at the Myron Williams store in Dexter.

Clabe sent to Sears, Roebuck for a Victrola, a little square box that played flat records, such as "Red Red Robin." He'd wind it up when he came in for noon dinner.

He bought a Model T for $700 and drove with Leora to the pasture to teach her to drive. The pasture was so lumpy that she'd get tickled. He finally gave up.

Neighbors commented on how straight Clabe's cornrows lined up, like railroad tracks.

After Clabe was done for the day in the field, he unhooked the plow, harrow, binder, or wagon from the horses. He led them to the water tank, but the horses made their own way to the barn and into their stalls where he unharnessed them, the leather making a slapping sound. Metal bits jingled; horses snorted. He pulled off the flynets, which had warded off the pests, from their backs. Ready to eat, all in a row, the sweaty teams, used to each other, were double-stalled.

Six-year-old Doris followed her dad into the barn, so Clabe handed her a three-pound coffee can and showed how much corn and oats to scoop out of the bin to feed the horses, or how many double handfuls of oats from the bushel basket, or how many ears of corn.

Clabe climbed into the mow and tossed hay with a pitchfork to the main floor, then forked it into the manger. Down the center of the barn was a box for grain at one end and a V-shaped box for hay. A cow was stalled with its own manger.

Being in the barn with her dad felt safe for a small girl, even with big farm animals munching nearby.

After the horses finished, they clopped to the pasture, then rolled to scratch their backs, feet flailing.

CHAPTER 58

Junior Wilson Born (1925)

Grandmother Goff's low voice early in the morning meant a new baby. Such an exciting time! Claiborne Junior Wilson was born July 6, 1925, at the Hemphill place, the first in the family born in Dallas County. It was so hot upstairs with no fans, so they all slept downstairs.

The Ringling Brothers circus came to Des Moines ten days later. Grandmother and Leora stayed home with the baby, two-year-old Danny, and the five-year-old twins, who'd be too hard to keep track of in a crowd.

The fairgoers were up before daybreak. The kids headed outside even before the roosters crowed. Leora fried chicken for their dinner, along with buttered bread. They drove the Model T to Des Moines. Once inside the circus area, Clabe told Doris to hang onto his finger so she wouldn't get lost.

They watched the circus animals in their cages before the big show started. Grandfather bought pop to share. With seats near the middle of the tent, they could watch the acts in all three rings. Back home, the boys could hardly wait to tell about the fat clown, who opened a door at the front of him and a little dog jumped in and came out at the back.

And when they got home, they had a new grandmother. Leora had given her a new modern haircut.

*L-R: Back: Delbert, Clabe holding Junior, Leora, Donald. Front: Danny, Dale,
Doris (her 7th birthday), Darlene. Near Dexter, August 30, 1925*

Junior Wilson, November 1925

On Christmas Eve, the Wilson children lined up their chairs in order of their ages, then hung a pair of socks, pinned together, over the back. On Christmas morning they'd find a box of unshelled nuts in one sock, mixed hard candy in the other. In the toe of one sock would hold a precious orange.

Their folks had ordered stiff paper boxes with Christmas scenes from Sears, Roebuck. Each arrived flat but the ends overlocked to form a suitcase shape, about 5-6 inches long, with a cord handle. Leora filled each with two or three pieces of hard ribbon candy and several with soft jelly-like centers. Dale saved his candy, making it last for weeks.

CHAPTER 59

Dale and Darlene Start School (1926)

The country kids ate dinner together at school, whatever their mothers had packed for them in metal pails. "What's that?" someone asked Doris. "It looks like blood!"

Leora had made tomato butter, then used it for sandwiches, just like apple butter. She always made whole wheat bread. Imagine slabs of bread with red stuff seeping out.

TOMATO BUTTER RECIPE

Cook peeled tomatoes down to puree. Add sugar and the slivered rind of oranges or lemons. Cook some more.

Clabe ate tomatoes with sugar and cream, just like his family did when he was growing up. Tastes "just like strawberries," he insisted.

In late autumn, the kids could smell piccalilli when they came home from school. The pungent aroma drew flies to the kitchen door, so Leora had the kids go around to the front door. They waited for her to unlock it and shoo the flies away with a dish towel.

Leora made piccalilli or chili sauce from chopped up vegetables and fruits from the end of her garden, with sugar, spices, and vinegar.

CHILI SAUCE (OR PICCALILLI)

1 peck ripe tomatoes

1/2 peck apples

1/4 peck onions

1 teaspoon cloves

1 teaspoon cinnamon

1 teaspoon allspice

2 tablespoons salt

1 quart vinegar

1 quart sugar

pepper - to suit taste (a red pepper is better)

Serve with any kind of meat.

Leora canned most of this concoction. Toward the end of the season, it included more apples.

Leora broke up meat and other foods in a metal grinder, which attached to the side of the table or counter. Food was pushed into a hopper, and someone cranked the handle to make it work. The bigger kids took turns. When Doris tried it, she realized it was arranged for a right-handed person. She worked around to the other side, vowing she could do better when she used her "father hand." She knew she'd said something clever.

L-R: Back: Delbert and Donald. Front: Dale and Darlene,
Junior (first birthday), Doris, Danny. July 6, 1926

Five sibling and the new and improved "Wilson school bus," November 1926

A home of their own, family nearby, getting healthy kids educated. Those were Leora's fondest wishes. By 1926, these grandchildren of Iowa pioneers were well on their way to fulfilling those dreams. Seven sturdy children, five of them in school, Clabe's job with a good income. Leora added to their income by raising chickens and now owned her own sewing machine.

With grandparents and cousins in town, they also had the blessing of family nearby.

All they'd lived through—loss of family members, a world war (then called the war to end all wars), surviving a pandemic, childhood diseases, a house fire, and all those moves. These forging episodes built their character, year by year. Together, Clabe and Leora were encouraged about the future.

Updates

CLABE'S GRANDFATHER, SAMUEL WILSON

Sam Wilson's story about living with Indians was borne out in the 1887 *Biographical and Historical Record of Green and Carroll Counties, Iowa*, published while Sam Wilson was still living.

LAURA'S TEACHER'S WATCH

Laura Jordan had a gold watch when she taught, but when she married, she traded the watch to her father for a cow. Her mother wore the watch, but when she died in 1914, Laura's father gave the watch back to his oldest daughter. Forty-eight years later, when Laura died, the watch was left to her oldest daughter, Leora. Leora gave the watch to her oldest daughter, Doris. My sister Gloria now owns the precious heirloom.

NORTHEAST NEBRASKA

My husband Guy and I visited this gently rolling Nebraska prairie with its wide-open sky in 2004. When we visited, thick clouds hovered but there was no hint of rain. The town of Bloomfield is about four blocks square, with a new city hall. On a Nebraska map you can find the town near the corner of the Santee Sioux reservation. We drove to Niobrara but couldn't find the GAR Hall where the Goff's Nebraska holdings were auctioned off in 1896.

Grandma Leora would be amused (but not surprised) to learn that her few clues to where she'd lived between the ages of three and six yielded enough information for us to visit Nebraska a hundred years after her father "went bust" there.

Northeast Nebraska suffered from drought in the 1890s, but during the spring of 2019, the same area was underwater.

THE LIZA JANE TRAIN

From *History of Menlo, Iowa: Gathering Steam for the Second Century, 1969*: "The branch train, called Liza Jane or Ol' Liza, to Guthrie Center was completed in 1880. She made two daily trips to Guthrie, carrying mail, express, and freight to Glendon, Monteith, and Guthrie. The train returned hauling hogs, cattle and grain for market. Menlo's turntable rotated Liza Jane for the second trip to Guthrie. Sometimes you could hear the engine after dark chug-chugging up the steep grade. Liza was housed at Stuart's roundhouse overnight."

Mom (Doris) and I spent part of a day in 1996 scouting out where they lived in Stuart during the 1920s, and hunting for the old railroad grade, where the *Liza Jane* journeyed through Guthrie County, Iowa, 1880-1958.

GRANDPAP AND GRANDMOTHER JORDANS' HOME, MONTEITH

Emelia Ann (Moore) Jordan's treasures included a vinegar cruet and a poppy plate, which the author owns today.

Emelia Jordan's poppy plate

KEY WEST, MINNESOTA

There wasn't much left of Key West when we visited in 2002, just a ramshackle elevator with a faint "KEY WEST, MINN." on the east side.

Key West elevator in 2002

The town had one house, a kind of community hall, and that's about all. The canals were still there—County Ditch 126 goes right through Key West—but the train tracks were gone.

1904 - Laura Goff bought the *Oxford Self-Pronouncing American Edition of the Holy Bible* while in Grand Forks, ND. I now am the keeper of that Bible, the one that comforted her when three sons served in WWI (their army numbers are listed inside), and which she read twice during the Great Depression.

THE DUROC JERSEY HOG "LAFOLLETTE"

Lafollette (#36563) is listed in *History of the Duroc-Jersey: Complete History from the Earliest Records of Red Hogs in America Down to the Present Time*, published in 1922. This hog was so famous that you can now even google "LaFollette 36563" and find him.

AUDUBON COUNTY

Leora's youngest brother, Virgil Cleon Goff, died just before his first birthday in 1909. He was buried in the Maple Grove Cemetery in Audubon, but there is a cenotaph for him, as well, in the Goff plot in Guthrie Center's Union Cemetery.

Leora Goff received a New Year card from Mrs. Donald J. Preston in December of 1909. What a shock it must have been for the 19-year-old to learn that Nora Isabel Brown-Preston died early the next month. This talented musician, gifted singer, and conductor of music for the public schools died three days after her baby son. Her funeral was held at the Presbyterian Church where she served as chorister. Nora Preston and her baby son are buried in Audubon.

PIANO

Leora took piano lessons and played the pump organ. Clabe bought a player piano for the family when they lived in Stuart, but by then they had six children. The piano didn't move to Dallas County with them. I don't think Leora had a piano for several decades. When Leora and her mother lived together in Guthrie Center after World War II, she bought a spinet piano. She enjoyed playing hymns, and watching grandchildren play it.

FROG POND SCHOOL

One of Clabe Wilson's schoolmates at Frog Pond School was Wesley Clampitt, who became the Superintendent of the Dexter School when Clabe's children attended there during the Great Depression. He is mentioned in *Leora's Dexter Stories.*

Part of the old foundation marks where
Frog Pond School stood (Photo thanks to Barry Branson)

WINDY GAP

Dirt road leading to Windy Gap as it looks today.

MRS. CONNRARDY'S SEWING SCHOOL

Old Connrardy house in Exira as it looks today. (Photo thanks to Susie Simpson, a great granddaughter of Alice B. Connrardy.)

THE ROGERS SILVERPLATE FROM CLABE

I've become the keeper of Clabe's Rogers silverplate, with oak leaves on the handles. The story of why there aren't many knives in the set is told in *Leora's Dexter Stories: The Scarcity Years of the Great Depression.*

LIBRARY TABLE

While the Goffs lived in the Victorian house, there were two oak mission-style library tables in the parlor. Doris played under them, lying across the shelf underneath. One of those tables moved from house to house with the Goffs, then the Wilsons. The heavy table returned to Guthrie Center where it held Leora's houseplants at 515 North 4th Street for four decades. It now holds a painted lamp in the front window of a great granddaughter in central Iowa.

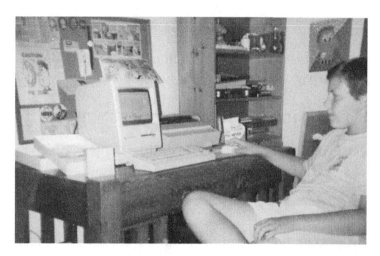

The library table from the Victorian house in Guthrie Center once held the Mac Plus in the room of Leora Wilson's great grandson, Dan Kidney.

THE GUTHRIE CENTER CHRISTIAN CHURCH

The Guthrie Center Christian Church, where Laura Goff "learned to vote," now houses the bell from the Monteith Church. Both Laura and daughter Leora worshiped there for decades.

Guthrie Center Christian Church

THE RETREAT

The Scottish Rite Park, a retirement home in Des Moines, was built on the site of The Retreat mental hospital.

THE "MORRISBURG CEMETERY" POEM

The poet, Nicholas Dowd, grew up in Guthrie Center. Clabe Wilson's mother and other relatives are buried in Morrisburg cemetery.

STUART

The three-story house from the Adventist Academy has been moved and remodeled. Mom and I saw the "Chittick house" shortly before it was torn down and replaced during the 1990s.

The Stuart Depot has been renovated and is in use for local activities. Commemorative bricks were sold as a fundraiser. Four Wilson bricks are part of the display near the depot.

The restored Stuart Depot as it looks today

WHITE POLE ROAD

Originally designated as White Pole Road in 1910 by an auto club, it followed the Chicago, Rock Island and Pacific Railroad from Des Moines to Council Bluffs. It promised a straighter, leveler and shorter route with a town every five to six miles. Poles along the route were painted white. Sometimes called the "Great White Way," in 1912, it was extended east to Davenport to the entire state. In 1914, it became the first certified route under Iowa State Highway Commission's rules.

Poles along a 26-mile stretch of the route, from Dexter to Adair, have been painted white once again, to connect five small towns for the purpose of development. Please see: http://www.white-poleroad.com.

The story of the paving of White Pole Road in 1929 is told in *Leora's Dexter Stories: The Scarcity Years of the Great Depression*.

LEORA'S HAIR

One flat box of Grandma Leora's keepsakes holds a swirl of her dark brown hair. She'd written about that historic haircut in her memoir.

The box with Leora's hair

The stories in *Leora's Early Years* have been woven from the memoirs of Leora (Goff) Wilson (family members have transcribed copies), World War I letters, newspaper clippings (some discovered on microfilm at the Iowa Historical Library, which meant having pizza at Noah's Ark as part of the outing with Doris, AKA Mom), postcards, Doris's stories, Delbert's stories, and travels to areas where Leora lived.

Questions to Ponder

How was life different for children when Leora was growing up? What did families do for entertainment? Would you have liked to grow up during those days?

Kem Luther, in *Cottonwood Roots*, said that Nebraska homesteaders knew there was "a line out there where the rain ended . . . We know today that this line twists its way through the heart of Nebraska like a rattlesnake . . . But when the droughts of the nineties came it was clear that the snaking line was a sidewinder . . ." Why were the Goffs and other pioneers so unaware of the problems they could encounter? Did the newspaper ads offer them a false hope?

What do you think about Sherd Goff's not allowing his older children to attend high school?

How would you compare women's lives then to now? Were some things better back then?

A study of 1741 cases of insanity by Edward Jarvis, published by the US Commissioner of Education in 1871, concluded that "over-study" was responsible for 205 of the insanity cases. He wrote, "Education lays the foundation of a large portion of the causes of mental disorder." How well do you think mental health was diagnosed and treated decades ago?

Do you suppose that Georgia Goff might have suffered from a brain tumor?

A person's character is forged during their early years as they go through the blacksmithing concepts of "heating and hammering." What might these early stories reveal about Leora's character, where it came from? What about Clabe?

What do you think happened in Georgia Wilson's first marriage? Why would she give up her first son so easily? Is it fair to conjecture this many years later?

Clabe and Leora's marriage may not have been "made in heaven," but what do you think made it work?

Acknowledgements

I'm so grateful for the generosity of my longest cheerleaders on this writing journey: Marilyn Bode, Jorja Dogic, Louise, Hartman, and Gloria Neal.

Elaine Briggs has been so helpful with ideas and suggestions. I'm a fan of her biography of her father, *Joe Dew: A Glorious Life*, and her new book, *Yes! All Can!*

Historian and genealogist Dave Anderson is the newest member of the team, correcting and sorting out those first few chapters.

How I've appreciated encouragement from members of the Dexter Museum Board: Doris Feller, Pat Hochstetler, Mary McCollogh, Gloria Neal, and Rod Stanley.

The willingness of these endorsers to give of their time and charitable words for *Leora's Early Years* has been such a blessing:

John Busbee, Founder of *The Culture Buzz*, Iowa Governor's Award for Partnership & Collaboration in the Arts, Iowa History Award for "Last Measure of Full Devotion," *Iowa History Journal*. He edited these last two "Leora Stories" and interviewed me about the first two for his radio program over KFMG-FM.

Arvid Husman, former newspaper publisher (my sister was always bringing home his delightful stories from *The Creston News Advertiser* when he was its publisher), regular columnist for *Iowa History Journal*, as well as several newspapers, author of *More Country Roads*.

Darcy Maulsby, MBA, 5th generation farmer, Iowa's Storyteller, author of several books, including *Madison County* and *A Culinary*

History of Iowa. She posts a photo of a cat each day, with a winsome caption, of Lieutenant Dan, Bonnie and Clyde, Dex (for Dexter), and a shy one named Bella.

Dennis L. Peterson, historian, author of several books, including *Look Unto the Hills: Stories of Growing Up in Rural East Tennessee,* and a regular contributor to *Our American Stories.*

Mark A. Peitzman, Historian and Preservationist, formerly with the State Historical Society of Iowa (SHSI) and the Iowa Dept. of Cultural Affairs (DCA). Mark is related to the Peitzman family who were so gracious to Clabe Wilson during the summer of 1935. The story is related in Chapter 31 of *Leora's Dexter Stories: The Scarcity Years of the Great Depression.*

Rod Stanley, historian, speaker, Guthrie County Historical Village and Museum Board, Dexter Museum Board. Rod recorded an interview for *Our American Stories* about the 1933 Shootout in Dexfield Park with Bonnie and Clyde Barrow.

Lee Habeeb, who readily agreed to write the foreword for *Leora's Early Years,* is the founder and host of *Our American Stories,* a talk radio executive, and Newsweek essayist. He is a University of Virginia Law School graduate and lives in beautiful Oxford, Mississippi. He is also humble, gracious, generous, and a delight to work with.

A big hug and thanks to Guy Kidney, chauffeur extraordinaire, for enduring perpetual stacks of papers and folders lying around, which eventually make their way into a blog post or even a book.

I thank all of you for joining me on this amazing and humbling journey to share more of Leora's stories.

About the Author

Joy Neal Kidney, Leora's oldest granddaughter, grew up on an Iowa farm and now lives in a Des Moines suburb with her husband, Guy, an Air Force Veteran of the Vietnam War and a retired Air Traffic Controller. Their son is married and they live out-of-state with a small daughter named Kate.

With God's help, Joy is aging gratefully. This graduate of the University of Northern Iowa has lived with fibromyalgia for two dozen years, giving her plenty of home-bound days to write blog posts and books. *Leora's Early Years: Guthrie County Roots* is her third book in the "Leora Stories" series. Her research from decades ago helps tell her grand-mother's stories.

She was presented with the 2021 Great American Storyteller Award "Honoring the woman who most beautifully tells the story of America to Americans," by *Our American Stories* and WHO NewsRadio 1040.

You may follow her on Twitter @ JoyNealKidney
on Instagram @ joynealkidney
and online at www.joynealkidney.com

With grit and determination, Leora keeps her dream alive of high school diplomas for her flock of seven children while dealing with emergencies and making a haven for the family in one run-down house after another.

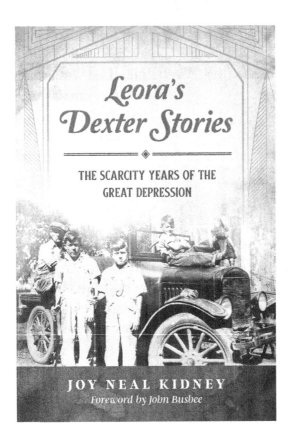

Hardbacks, paperbacks, and ebooks are available from Amazon.com.

Autographed and shipped paperbacks are available from Beaverdale Books, Des Moines. (515) 279-5400, beaverdalebooks@gmail.com

Five brothers served. Only two came home.

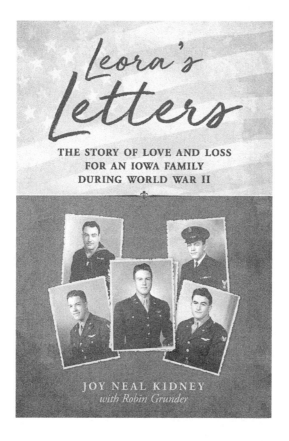

Hardbacks, paperbacks, ebooks, and audiobooks are available from Amazon.com

Autographed and shipped paperbacks are available from Beaverdale Books, Des Moines. (515) 279-5400, beaverdalebooks@gmail.com

Made in the USA
Monee, IL
03 September 2024

65095448R00146